EVENTING
INSIGHTS

BLYTH TAIT, MBE

World Champion

KENILWORTH PRESS

The Kenilworth Press Ltd
Addington
Buckingham
MK18 2JR

British Library Cataloguing in Publication Data
A catalogue record for this book is available from
the British Library.

ISBN 1-872082-70-X Paperback
(ISBN 1-872082-45-9 Hardback)

Text design: Paul Saunders
Line drawings: Maggie Raynor
Layout and typesetting: Kenilworth Press Ltd
Printed and bound in Great Britain by
Hillman Printers (Frome) Ltd

FRONTISPIECE *Messiah, jumping into the lake at
Badminton, 1990, on his way to second place.*

EVENTING INSIGHTS

BLYTH TAIT, MBE

World Champion

KENILWORTH PRESS

The Kenilworth Press Ltd
Addington
Buckingham
MK18 2JR

British Library Cataloguing in Publication Data
A catalogue record for this book is available from
the British Library.

ISBN 1-872082-70-X Paperback
(ISBN 1-872082-45-9 Hardback)

Text design: Paul Saunders
Line drawings: Maggie Raynor
Layout and typesetting: Kenilworth Press Ltd
Printed and bound in Great Britain by
Hillman Printers (Frome) Ltd

*FRONTISPIECE Messiah, jumping into the lake at
Badminton, 1990, on his way to second place.*

CONTENTS

ACKNOWLEDGEMENTS

Grateful thanks go to my parents, Glenise and Bob, for buying me that first pony to share with my sisters. Since then their support and encouragement have been unwaivering.

Many thanks also to my generous owners who have completely entrusted their horses to me and always accepted my decisions unquestioningly.

Over the years many have worked hard in the background while I have hogged the limelight, but particular thanks must go to Delayne Cooke, Paul O'Brien and Fiona Tibone, for sticking with me through the good times as well as the bad.

Special thanks are due to Philip Billington, Margrit Key and Toggi Ltd for their timely input and subsequent continued involvement.

And, finally, without the typists Chrys Cochrane, Julie Ashby and Sue Williams, who deciphered my scribbled notes, and editor Lesley Gowers of Kenilworth Press, this book would never have reached fruition.

PREFACE

Whoever coined the phrase 'There's more than one way to skin a cat,' could not have spoken a truer word. In writing this book I would not even begin to suggest that the techniques described should be taken as gospel nor that they represent the only recipe for producing event horses and competing successfully in horse trials.

What follows is simply an insight into the methods behind my madness. Throughout I have tried to be perfectly honest and tell it exactly as it is, rather than how it should be, to show what is ordinarily possible.

Undoubtedly many will disagree with some of the things I have to say, but I readily appreciate that my methods will not suit every rider or every horse. I have simply written down what has worked for me and allowed me to enjoy a certain amount of success from time to time.

If, through the pages that follow, aspiring riders can capitalise on my learning experiences, then I feel the exercise of writing this book will have been worthwhile.

FACING PAGE
Messiah, back home after winning the 1990 World Championships.

1

WINNING IS BELIEVING

———————— • ————————

I GUESS it must be possible that some people are more naturally suited to three-day eventing than others, but even so I strongly believe that successful competition riders are in fact made and not born. Sure, some riders' chances are substantially enhanced by their background, but ultimately it takes much more than just one good horse or ample financial providence to be consistently successful.

Far more important is a strong personal desire to do well. A healthy competitive spirit will encourage total determination and dedication towards improving performance. It is primarily what lies within a rider's mind that will dictate his eventual limits of achievement and will govern to what degree a rider obtains his goals.

Likewise, all event riders must possess a really genuine love of horses to even consider being involved in horse trials, for it is common knowledge that disappointments and failures will inevitably outnumber the rare moments of glory. Many hours will be spent in the sole company of just one horse, in all kinds of weather, and often at the expense of a normal social life. Nevertheless eventing can be an exciting sport with many satisfying rewards.

Some folks participate purely and simply for enjoyment, and these people are a very welcome and important part of the infrastructure of the sport. Most of these riders never aspire to compete beyond, say, a novice three-day event or an intermediate horse trials, but they are indeed an invaluable asset to eventing and are much admired and applauded by the likes of myself.

However, nowadays such is the level of professionalism at the top end of the sport that any rider wishing to succeed beyond just the initial introductory levels must be prepared to focus his

FACING PAGE
Delta stretches out over a spread.

11

Before the start of the cross-country is a time for focusing mental attitude towards a positive performance and coping with competition nerves. Kristina Gifford at Burghley.

intentions totally very early on in his career.

I know for certain that if I was unable to compete at high-level three-day eventing, participating in major competitions, then I probably wouldn't be interested in riding simply for pleasure. I am a highly competitive person and need strong goals to provide the necessary motivation to sustain the amount of effort required. For this reason, winning is of some significance to me. It is not all-consuming, but without the desire to achieve or come out on top, I feel that my performance would suffer as a result of being more easily contented by just a satisfactory showing. The desire to be the best serves to provide the incentive to constantly improve my technique, thereby (I hope) bettering my performance all the time. Without this I would be merely offering others the competitive edge.

We are lucky that our sport shows no mercy to those who develop over-inflated egos. Horses are the best of levellers. It is quite possible to be a big winner one day and end up flat on the floor the next, which explains why eventing is a sport which can still boast a strong camaraderie amongst its participants. Everybody knows that pride comes before a fall, and although we are matched against one another we are also united in our challenge against the courses, the elements and the myriad problems that present themselves.

I believe that the right mental attitude holds the key to a top performance and if a rider is not fortunate enough to possess an

Don't dwell on the occasions when things go wrong - just get back on board and keep kicking. Remounting Delphy Dazzle after falling at Montacute, 1991.

ideal temperament naturally then he must learn to develop one.

First and foremost I feel it is extremely important to be positive and confident in what you are trying to do. A negative attitude will just not do. Never allow self-doubt to creep into a performance for it will have a detrimental effect on the way you ride: instead of being determined and attacking you will begin to think about being defensive and playing safe. Looking back on the times in the past when my performances have suffered most, and even during the times when I contemplated giving up, I can nearly always place the blame on being negative. Often, though, there were reasons - for example, I might have known that the preparation for a particular competition had been most unsatisfactory or insufficient - but, having said that, once the competition is under way the name of the game is to get on and forget the past.

Even in training I am sure it is better to be doing the wrong thing with one hundred per cent conviction than it is to be doing the right thing in a half-hearted manner. The results will invariably be more constructive.

Building up towards the World Championships in 1990 my confidence was at an all-time high. The preparation had gone extremely well with no major set-backs, so I moved onwards with growing positive intentions. It is true that success breeds confidence, and following a good second at Badminton, I even began to entertain thoughts that I could win. But, in stark contrast, during the run-up to the Barcelona Olympic Games in 1992 I did not possess that same positive mental attitude because I was not confident about my preparation. It had been necessary for Messiah to have nearly a whole year off due to an injury caused by a blow to a foreleg. He returned to competition fresh and disobedient, resulting in frequent disagreements between rider and horse. Time was not on our side, and as the Games drew nearer the pressure continued to escalate. I was all too aware of my weaknesses at that time and tended to focus too sharply upon them. Interestingly those negative fears related mainly to the dressage phase. Once the worst that could happen had indeed happened the rest of the competition revealed a total reversal of form because of an equivalent U-turn in mental attitude. I would almost go so far as to say that in an imaginary equation for successful performance mental attitude would outweigh physical input in a ratio of about two to one.

Relaxation is also important, both in training and in competition, as very little is ever achieved in a state of panic or by making hasty

In the ten-minute box, Saumur, 1992. I prefer to distance myself from the surrounding activities to mull over any last-minute information and plan my attack.

decisions. Tension is very easily communicated to a horse, so a rider must try to stay calm at all times. This is not always easy to do at competitions, but you can help matters considerably by ensuring that your immediate environment offers you exactly what you need. For example, if you are a person who needs support and bolstering then make sure you are surrounded by the right type of people. An over-protective and excitable mother is therefore best kept out of the ten-minute box. I like to be left mostly to myself to work things out in my head. Before a competition begins I like to have plenty of time to plan out the day's happenings and prefer not to be bothered or rushed.

At home, when schooling, a relaxed mind is also a pre-requisite. Horses do not reason well and do not understand anger tantrums from a rider who has lost his cool. They learn much more readily from constant and consistent repetition.

If a rider ever starts to become unduly worried about hurting himself then it is definitely time to give up. We are all concerned about making mistakes and losing face by a stupid stop or run-out but if we are preoccupied by a fear of getting injured then we really shouldn't be eventing. The sport is physically demanding, but if approached sensibly, it becomes less risky. It is also important for the rider to be physically fit so that he does not jeopardise his horse's chances. By riding several horses every day I find that I achieve a level of fitness that is usually satisfactory. However, if I

Having a trainer to help with the final preparation can boost confidence. It's never too late to learn. Working in with Hans Erik Pedersen.

was preparing to ride two horses at Badminton, for example, then I would probably undertake some supplementary exercise. I find jogging, swimming and cycling to be the most helpful.

Quite often we are faced with fences towards the end of the course that have to be ridden with control and accuracy, and it is over these obstacles that so many riders make errors in judgment, simply because they are too exhausted to make the necessary adjustments. This is especially true if the horse has been pulling hard and is a handful for the rider to manage. Similar fences placed at the beginning of the course, when the rider is fresh, can normally be negotiated successfully so it is a matter of professionalism for the rider to ensure that his physical fitness does not jeopardise his own or his horse's safety. Luckily I have never had to worry about my weight, but if I was overweight I would be concerned about disadvantaging my chances and would make a concerted effort to diet.

Once the correct mental attitude is established then technique can simply be learnt. The more enquiring the mind, then the easier this task will become. I like to receive as much tuition as possible, from a wide variety of sources. I always try to listen to what is being offered, and after trial and error and thoroughly digesting the information I adapt it to my own style, but only if I feel it is right for me. It is a shame for riders to lose totally their own natural style and flair, because once the competition has begun the ability to ride instinctively and be self-reliant must come entirely from within the rider.

Much of what I have been taught I have eventually chosen not to incorporate into my own style as I feel it unsuitable to me personally. However, I never feel that I can stop learning nor that I know it all. Readiness to change and accept new ideas is very important if we are to keep up with the play. I particularly like to watch other riders as often as possible, both in training and in competition, as I find observation a very useful learning tool. Trying to work out why a certain rider applies a certain technique can be very educational.

2

THE RIGHT HORSE

———————— • ————————

JUST as in mathematics where we are taught that one exception to a rule can disprove a theory, so with horses it is difficult to try and standardise a single formula for finding the perfect eventer. Numerous star performers from the past have shown us that success comes in all shapes, sizes, colours and breeds. Thankfully, different things appeal to different folks ensuring that we will continue to see a diverse range of competition horses, but basically in all of these star performers we have been able to recognise at least some similar qualities: namely those of courage, athleticism and strength of character, to pinpoint but a few.

Although we all have our own preferences and pre-conceived ideas of what we are looking for in our own potential champions, I always try to approach each new recruit with an open mind in order to judge the animal on its individual merits.

Much is often made of the importance of good conformation and it is true that this will have a significant bearing on the general soundness and all-round likelihood of future success. However, I personally place the greatest emphasis on the correct mental attitude. This is much more than just a suitable temperament. I am ultimately looking for a performance horse, so if the mind is not willing then the perfect conformation of a show-ring winner will be of no consequence to me.

Remembering the relative importance of the cross-country on the eventual outcome of our multi-disciplined sport, I always choose a horse most suited to that particular phase. I look for one that shows a real desire to run and jump, a genuine love for tackling natural obstacles, and (importantly) a wish to please. Unfortunately it is not

King Boris, ridden by Mary Thomson, is typical of a heavier-built event horse. His clever-ness and agility across country brought him many successes.

always possible to detect these qualities immediately, but quite often first impressions will indicate much of what is in store.

A perky, bright-eyed expression, with ears alert and an interested outlook, is more preferable to me than a blank stare or scowling face. Likewise, I have now grown weary of horses that constantly 'rest' a hind leg when being groomed or handled as it usually signifies an unwillingness to participate or even actual laziness. Whereas I might accept a horse with a minor physical imperfection that

Who would want a chestnut warmblood mare? I would, if it was Feine Dame - silver medallist at the Barcelona Olympics. Judge each horse on its individual merits not on any preconceptions.

would not be detrimental to its general soundness, I would immediately reject one that displayed an obvious reluctance or a lack of intelligence.

Always bear in mind the suitability of the horse you choose to complement your own personal circumstances and level of experience. For novice level one-day eventing, nearly any type of horse could be suitable, but for top-level three-day competitions it is becoming increasingly evident that quality animals of near pure blood are required, otherwise they may not possess the necessary speed and stamina.

Being slightly built I am best suited to a lighter-framed, quick-thinking and quick-moving horse such as the New Zealand thoroughbred. My sights are always set firmly on the major championship tracks where a limitless supply of energy and total commitment are absolutely vital. But not everybody aspires to participate in the Olympic Games, and so for a novice or part-time rider who is not able to spend long hours in the saddle on a daily basis, a horse with a gentle nature and relaxed temperament should be a prerequisite.

Follow your own basic instincts with regard to size, colour, breed and type of character, as compatibility with you personally will be required, but on matters of mechanical structure it is advisable to seek some knowledgeable assistance. It is very easy for the uneducated to unwittingly overlook small conformational faults that may prove the horse's undoing in time.

I look for a horse that appears to stand naturally square. Having a foot in each corner, as the old saying goes, indicates to me a natural balance.

Ideally the horse should show a well-rounded top-line from poll to tail. Often this can be improved with correct schooling, especially if a good frame is there in the first place. I have found, though, that in most cases where serious depletions of correct muscle occur, it tends to be as a result of a defect in skeletal construction. Take, for example, Ra Ora, a young horse of mine who is ewe-necked (see photo on page 25). To an extent, the problem is being slowly rectified with schooling. However, as with so many ewe-necked horses, his training has been more difficult. If a horse tends to carry his head high then it is likely that he will move in an inverted fashion and possibly even jump in a hollow outline. In Ra Ora's instance, the problem seems to stem from straighter than normal hocks, and his reluctance to use them to propel himself effectively. He much prefers to pull himself along with his forehand, pushing his head up in the process. I continue to persevere with him because he is excellent in all other respects, already boasting an enviable performance record that includes completing his first international three-day event and moving up to advanced grade without ever having incurred a single

(*Above*) *Messiah and* (*below*) *Delta, both horses measuring 16hh and by the same sire (Aberlu). Messiah is built for the job: he is well put together, athletic, and stands balanced with a naturally rounded top-line. Delta is a compact mare, a little less streamlined. Her shoulder is a fraction straighter and her neck set on a little lower, both factors which are reflected in her movement. Both horses have good, well-proportioned limbs.*

cross-country or show-jumping penalty.

It is important that the front and back halves of a horse match each other in type and size. A large, powerful hindquarter matched with a low wither and short neck will result in a constant downhill ride; just as a high forehand and generous length of rein, coupled with a chopped-off, weak hindquarter will produce a lack of driving power.

I have yet to encounter a really good horse that did not possess a proportionally deep girth. There must be room to house the motor (the heart). Likewise a wide, full chest will better accommodate the all-important lung space.

Whenever I look at a horse, the shoulders, perhaps more than any other part of the horse's anatomy, frequently come under greatest criticism. I want to see ample slope and length, as upright shoulders will cause undue concussion on the forelegs and can also produce shortened paces.

I like to give the limbs careful consideration when inspecting a new horse. The legs, particularly the front ones, will need to take most of the wear and tear from the strains of galloping and the impact of drop landings, and endure the inevitable bumps and bangs which result from jumping fixed timber fences. A generous amount of bone is therefore desirable, but not too much or the horse may be too heavy to travel long distances at speed. Most New Zealand thoroughbreds, including my own horses, lack a little in their amount of bone, but as they are born into the paddock and spend most of their formative years running naturally in outdoor surroundings and over varied terrain, their limbs develop early, producing rugged, tough legs. I would certainly not want a horse to have spindly legs or to be too long in the cannon bone as such an individual would be unlikely to stand up to the rigours of horse trials. I will sometimes tolerate a splint or a curb, as long as it is not too large in size or in a position where it could cause further aggravation.

Good, well-shaped and proportionately sized joints are necessary, and I would most definitely shy away from a horse that was 'back at the knee'. In an event horse this is a serious fault as it will distribute the bodyweight unequally to the back of the leg giving rise to the possibility of injury to the supporting ligaments and tendons. A horse that is slightly forward at the knee is a little more acceptable than the above, and I have actually found that these horses tend to make quite good jumpers, folding effectively with their front legs.

Upright pasterns, like long sloping ones, are undesirable for quite opposite reasons. Short, upright pasterns will not absorb the concussive effect of hard ground and long sloping ones will transfer most of the strain to the back of the leg - like long cannon bones these are seen as a sign of weakness.

'No foot, no horse' is all too true. I always look for strong, well-rounded hooves since these are vital. Regrettably, Messiah's most obvious conformational defect is in his feet. Because he is very upright all round and especially on the inside of both front feet, this has resulted in a slight turning out of his hooves. With regular and very careful corrective shoeing, and also ensuring that not too much wall is allowed to grow at a faster rate on the outside to unbalance his weight-bearing surface areas, the problems have been slightly reduced and long-term repercussions avoided. Personally, I am always suspicious of clumsy-looking, over-sized, 'pudding bowl' feet.

Unfortunately good movement is not always immediately recognisable, unless of course it is obviously very extravagant. I do believe, though, that it is often the biggest-moving horses - the ones who possess floating, foot-flicking trot steps - who turn out to be the most careless show jumpers. Sometimes loose movement below the knee can carry through to the horse's jumping technique. Good fore-arm movement and slightly higher knee action, although less impressive from a dressage viewpoint, can normally indicate a more natural jumping technique. Having said that, though, a short, choppy stride is also far from desirable if we are to produce the elasticity to display the medium and extended paces that are required in advanced level tests.

Much emphasis should be placed on the ability to gallop if three-day event aspirations are in mind. When trying a horse for possible purchase I am never frightened to ask the seller if I may try a horse at gallop. Sometimes the findings can be surprising in that they can disappoint or please. Delta is a horse who does not possess a good natural canter, finding it very difficult to engage sufficiently when collected. Much of this is could be attributable to the portion of standardbred or trotting blood thought to be in her mother's pedigree. She does, however, possess an enormous galloping stride, generated by her powerful hindquarters and strong hocks.

To some extent, the walk will sometimes offer a hint as to what the horse's gallop will be like. A swinging movement, where the hind feet overstep the footprints of the front feet, might suggest that

Ra Ora is younger than Messiah and Delta with less muscle development. His top-line is not well rounded as he shows a slight ewe neck and a less powerful rump. He does possess an exceptionally deep girth and big chest and although he stands a couple of inches taller (16.2hh) his limbs are comparatively short. This is desirable in a jumper.

the horse will gallop well.

When purchasing any new horse I am normally restricted by the amount of money I have to spend. Nevertheless I am mindful of the fact that it can be a false economy to buy a cheap horse, and with it a bundle of troubles that can be expensive to put right. Having decided that I like the look and type of a particular horse, as well as his attitude, I will ask to see it trotted up in hand and then in action. It can be a good idea to watch the owner riding the horse to assess whether it has been well trained or developed any peculiarities because of the way it has been produced. It will also give you a chance to observe the horse's movement, presence and jumping technique.

Although I always give a prospective horse a thorough work-out, I don't feel it is necessary to make the trial unduly strenuous. I like to ask for a little walk, trot and canter before moving on to more complicated manoeuvres. Basically if the horse shows natural balance and a receptive brain then it's up to me to produce the rest - provided that the horse isn't supposedly 'made'.

I am always a little suspicious of pre-arranged jump layouts, because I suspect that these are designed to show off the horse's best points and never its worst. I tend therefore to move jumps around, trying out an assortment of small gymnastic exercises. Also, if I am sure I am not going to ruin a horse's confidence, nor upset the owner, I like to pop the horse over one decent-sized fence to test his scope and courage. Normally twice will be enough, with particular attention being paid to the second effort. If the horse repeats a mistake, he would lose points for intelligence and respect.

If offered the chance to jump a few small cross-country fences I would certainly take it, and would probably finish off the trial with a short gallop.

In the end it is the horses I 'click' with immediately that invariably prove to be the long-term winners. There has to be a rapport between horse and rider if the partnership is to be ultimately successful. Funnily enough, though, Messiah, Delta and Tempo found me, rather than the other way round.

3

A QUESTION OF TECHNIQUE

———————— • ————————

ON MANY occasions I have heard three-day event riders being referred to as 'Jacks of all trades', and it is indeed true that in order to be continually successful in this sport, a rider must show the flexibility to be equally proficient in the three disciplines of dressage, show jumping and cross-country. However, where some people seem to make their single biggest mistake is that their technique or training lacks a common thread that runs consistently throughout the three phases. We cannot expect our horses to operate in three completely different ways, so logically we should not try to ride them in three diverse styles.

I feel it would be wrong to think of any one phase as a single entity in itself or as a means to an end for fear of creating confusion in my own mind or, worse still, in my horse's. I therefore try to follow a pattern that will allow me to adapt my position around a central theme, accordingly modified to suit a particular discipline and yet still complementing the other two phases. At one end of the scale the dressage position will be upright with the seat deep in order to effectively create the necessary collected impulsion and control, and at the other end, a more forward and light seat is needed to accommodate the increased speed of galloping - but always the twin ideals of being evenly weighted over the centre of balance and of riding sympathetically forward from the leg into the hand in an uncomplicated manner are sought.

For the dressage it is important that the rider should develop a deep seat and sit well into and around the horse in order that the combination should become one and therefore work in harmony and not at odds. The entire weight of the rider should be as evenly

The dressage position - sitting upright and tall in the saddle, with a good length of stirrup. An imaginary vertical line could be drawn through shoulder, hip and heel. The elbow could be more bent and the hands held higher to create another imaginary line dissecting elbow, hands and bit.

distributed over the horse's centre of balance as possible. Subsequently the upper body should be upright immediately above the seat with the legs stretched long directly beneath. The rider should always be relaxed, not stiff or tense, and it is important that he does not grip too much with the thigh and knee or else he will be squeezed upwards against the natural movement of the horse. Also, with the weight blocked in the thigh and knee, the lower leg, which is responsible for communicating so many commands to the horse, will be weakened.

I find it necessary to work frequently without stirrups in order to check and correct any faults in my position. As an event rider it is all too easy to tip the upper body forward without realising, because of all the jumping, hacking and galloping that we do. This will prevent the correct use of back and seat aids in dressage. Working without stirrups makes leaning forward awkward as the seat tends to keep bouncing out of the saddle without the weight of the upper body directly above it to act as an anchor. Also, without stirrups I tend to lose stiffness and tension by sinking into the movement more, relaxing and simply allowing my legs to hang down naturally. This has the effect of putting the seat deeper into the saddle, giving added security.

I find it is a good idea to envisage two imaginary lines: one that runs vertically through our body, dissecting our shoulder, hip and heel; and another that runs horizontally, dissecting our elbows, hands and the horse's mouth. Any break in these lines should be avoided. For example, if the hands are held below the withers, breaking the horizontal line, a pulley effect will be created and, despite the rider's wishes, will probably cause the horse's head to come up in resistance.

In achieving a correct riding position the rider's arms and hands are extremely important and their control is often the bane of many a rider. I try to imagine that my arms are just an extension of the reins and that they are also very elastic, which conjures up an impression that I can easily give and retake the contact freely and sympathetically. In an endeavour to engage the horse's hocks and put him on the bit, it is easy to fall into the trap of locking the elbows and fixing the hands, and in so doing actually create resistance in the horse's mouth.

In most of our everyday activities, when we are not riding horses, we tend to watch our hands in whatever we are doing - be it preparing food, using scissors or cleaning tack. Consequently when we are mounted it is difficult to draw the focus of our eyes away from our hands - however, we must. Whether it be riding a straight line, prescribing a circle or executing a half-pass, the rider must look straight ahead where he intends to go and not down at what his hands are doing. Instead the rider must develop a 'feel'. Looking down will only confuse our direction and stop us from riding positively forward. Looking ahead will always allow the rider to be better prepared and therefore ride more accurately.

Likewise, the rider's shoulders should always be positioned squarely above the horse's shoulders. When not moving on a straight line, this is achieved by slightly turning the hips to face the direction of the movement. For example, when making a circle the outside shoulder should be slightly more forward than the inside one, just as would be the case for the horse. When turning, the inside hip should not collapse nor should the inside shoulder drop lower, but the weight should still remain evenly distributed over both seat bones.

When applying the aids I always try to remember this simple sequence of application: firstly, the back and seat, then the legs and finally the hands. This will ensure that the desire to move forward is always maintained. Frequently this sequence is carried out in reverse, resulting in the horse exhibiting resistance or a complete reluctance to move forward and engage the hindquarters correctly.

The same basic principles follow through into our jumping, but as the centre of balance shifts slightly more forward as the movement becomes less collected, so too will our position. As the stride opens up, and to accommodate for the jumping effort, our stirrup will need to be shortened in order to support us so that we will not get left behind. We can no longer remain seated in the saddle whilst the horse is jumping, so in order to be ready I like to ride with a lightened seat between the fences, finding the security in the lower leg instead. This factor is further emphasised during the cross-country phase, where we will be required to negotiate many varied gradients and undulations, and obviously we will want to avoid banging around on the horse's back, which will slow him down or cause him to tire.

By riding as much as possible from the leg into the hand in the show jumping and leaving the seat to be used mainly in the dressage, we will become better equipped for the cross-country too. By relying on our seat too much in the show jumping we will not only weaken our leg but will find it necessary to be over active with our body movement when the horse actually jumps. If a rider is sitting

Stirrup length for show jumping (left) and for cross-country (right). The stirrup is longer for the show jumping to allow the rider to remain close to the saddle. For cross-country the angle of the knee is more closed and the stirrup shorter to absorb increased speed and varied gradients. Also the rider's leg is more forward in the cross-country position.

bolt upright in the approach to a fence, using a lot of back and seat at the point of take-off, he must then literally throw himself forward and play 'catch up' to avoid being left behind the movement. This can have the adverse effect of causing the horse to dive forward instead of backing off and taking time to round over the top rail. Even if the rider is lucky enough not to dislodge the top pole he will probably find a whole new set of problems on landing. The horse might be strong and flat, making it difficult to regain the control in time for the next fence. Nowadays, with the increasingly technical problems of related distances, it is important that the rider is balanced on landing as well as over the fence and on take-off.

I suggest that the rider should remain still with the upper body during the approach, over the fence and when riding away from the fence, and that he should not exaggerate the shoulder thrust or hip folding. Eventers are only required to jump fences that do not exceed three feet eleven inches in height so we can leave the aerial acrobatics to the Grand Prix jumpers and concentrate more on establishing an even and rhythmical balance. If the upper body can remain roughly at an angle of about forty-five degrees then the rider, with his weight well down into his heel and his seat light, needs only to offer the hand forward in a 'crest release' over the fence to give the horse sufficient freedom to execute a good bascule. Remember, it only takes a little body movement to upset a horse's balance.

I always offer my crest release along the horse's neck rather than by reaching down and forward on each side of the neck, to prevent myself from getting in front of the movement. Also this avoids the temptation to lower the shoulders too much when lowering the hands, which in turn can cause a pivot to be created in the knee and as a result the lower leg slips back.

An exercise I use a lot when preparing to jump and when teaching other riders, is to warm up in what I call a two-point position. Imagining the three main points of contact with the horse to be the seat, the knee and the heel, I will completely abandon the first point of contact, my seat, thereby transferring my entire weight one hundred per cent onto my stirrup. This helps to strengthen the effectiveness of the lower leg and to establish a secure independent position. If balance cannot be maintained in trot and canter then it is likely that independence over the fence will not be there either without the reliance of the hand on the horse's mouth. If I constantly topple forwards onto the horse's neck then I know I need to move my leg up to the girth and underneath me for base support. Or if I

The rider's position when show jumping

(a) At the moment before take-off the rider's weight is taken on the stirrup and the seat is light. The upper body is at a 45 degree angle and the eyes are looking ahead.

(c) On landing, the weight is still taken on the stirrup and the hands move back again to resume the control.

(b) Whilst in the air, the upper body should remain still, with the weight well down into the heel. The hand offers forward in a crest release, which allows the horse the freedom to lower his head and neck. This crest release should be executed along the neck rather than down each side to prevent the rider's shoulders from pitching too low, which in turn can cause the lower leg to slip back as the rider pivots on the knee.

(d) In the first stride after landing, just as in the approach, the upper body remains at a 45 degree angle, the seat is light and the rider is ready for the next fence.

A useful exercise for strengthening the lower leg and developing a balanced jumping seat is to work on the flat in a two-point position. This will redistribute the rider's weight one hundred per cent onto the stirrup and encourage independence.

fall backwards into the saddle with my seat then probably my legs are too far forward. I will also work in this two-point position when going up or down hill out hacking to further strengthen the leg and find my own security and balance, despite the changes in the horse's centre of balance.

Also when practising the two-point position in my flatwork preparation for jumping I will perform some transitions, both upwards and downwards, making sure that I can remain in balance and that the horse will respond to my leg without the associated use of my seat. I find it surprising that many riders cannot perform a canter strike-off without sitting into the saddle and driving rather than simply applying the lower leg.

When in the ring during the show-jumping phase, the closeness of my seat with the saddle is regulated by the length of the stride. The more open and free the stride, the less contact. If I am executing a hairpin or tight turn, I will sink down and bring the shoulders back slightly as the stride is collected and the centre of balance moves back, and use the seat as an additional aid for maintaining impulsion. But otherwise, and always when approaching a fence, I prefer to ride 'light'. Then during moments of extreme loss of impulsion, when for example a horse might back off excessively from, say, a water tray or spooky fence, then I have my seat to call upon as extra ammunition.

When it comes to the cross-country phase then the most obvious difference between that and the show jumping is that if the horse or rider makes a serious mistake then it is usually not the fence that will end up on the ground. Accordingly, although the rider must be positive and attacking in his technique, safety and self-preservation must always be uppermost in his mind.

Basically the rider's position on the approach to cross-country

Even when attacking cross-country fences I tend to think defensively. After all, solid timber obstacles don't fall if you hit them so I modify my position slightly for self-preservation. My shoulders will remain more upright, avoiding the possibility of being caught in front of the movement. I don't offer the same crest release as when show jumping because I like to retain a feel on the horse's mouth at all times in case of mishap. Messiah, World Championships, Stockholm, 1990.

jumps will be similar to that adopted in the show jumping, i.e. using a light seat and strong leg into a controlling hand right until the point of take-off. But once airborne then the position will modify slightly to compensate for the unforgiving nature of the fixed fences.

I allow my lower leg to move fractionally more forward on take-off than is normally considered conventional. This is designed to counteract the possibility of a sudden check of the forward momentum should a slight mistake be made by the horse. Bearing in mind that the horse has not had the luxury of a course walk, it is quite possible that he may misinterpret a fence or be surprised by what lies beyond it and give the timber a rub with his front legs. The faster the speed then the more this heel-forward rule needs to be enforced.

The stirrup will already have been shortened slightly from the show-jumping length, because with the increased speed the centre of balance will have moved forward again. I have the holes in my stirrup leathers spaced quite closely together to allow for small adjustments to be made. Normally I take my stirrups up three holes to ensure that the angle in the knee is sufficient to allow me to

Ginny Leng, demonstrating all the attributes of a safe cross-country position: weight well into the stirrup; seat close to the saddle; shoulders up, reducing the chances of being caught ahead of the movement; and a good rein

In order not to be dislodged by the impact of landing, the weight should always be taken on the stirrup. This in turn will allow the horse to regain stability. Here, on Shady Lane, I have slipped my reins during the drop into the water but without abandoning the contact altogether. The reins will be gathered up again in time for the exit fence.

absorb the variations in terrain and yet still feel secure. For the steeplechase phase at a three-day event, I would go up one or two holes again from my cross-country length, but basically the length of the rider's leg will influence how many holes the stirrup will need to be shortened. It is more common to see riders attempting to cope with stirrups that are too long than too short.

When going across country it is better to be slightly behind the movement as the horse jumps rather than precariously caught in front at any time. Consequently I tend to keep my shoulders more upright than most when negotiating solid timber and will sometimes slip my reins slightly so that I don't risk being pulled forward. I'm not sure if this defence mechanism has evolved from riding extravagant-jumping horses such as Messiah and Delta or from the painful experiences of being ejected out the front door when learning.

Sometimes, in order not to get caught ahead of the movement, it may be necessary to move the shoulders back even further, as is the case when negotiating drops and jumps into water. When this happens it will be necessary to slip the reins considerably so as not to interfere with the horse's balance. Nevertheless I always try to maintain a feel on the horse's mouth, so that in the event of an emergency such as a stumble or peck I can immediately assist the horse to regain his feet. Even when galloping between obstacles I would never lose the contact on the horse's mouth for fear of a slip.

The impact of landing should always be taken on the stirrup and not on the horse's back or the rider will be bounced off unceremoniously. Likewise, when galloping the weight should be off the horse's back leaving the horse free to gallop. Even when approaching fences I teach my pupils to sit up by all means to gain control but to try not to sit down. There is no better way to tire a horse or slow its progress than by sitting on it. The rider should be able to use the leg to generate impulsion. If it were just a matter of having a strong seat then surely the heavier the rider the more effective he would be. This is not the case.

4

ENTER AT A...

———————•———————

LIKE MANY other 'hot-blooded' event riders, I have found dressage the most difficult phase with which to come to grips. In fact, initially I found the idea of producing even a half-respectable test completely overwhelming and impossibly daunting. However, by slowly beginning to understand some of the basic objectives of dressage training I have begun to enjoy flatwork schooling more and even to experience the occasional rewarding moment.

Although I was always fully aware of the need to get off to a good start with a polished performance in phase one if a high over-all placing was to be achieved on day three, it was considerably less obvious, earlier on, just how much more efficient and effective the cross-country and show-jumping rounds would become with a better schooled, better balanced and more responsive horse at my command. With the increased technicality of modern cross-country courses, the emphasis is now more on the ability of the rider to communicate easily with his horse in order to successfully negotiate the problems of distance, accuracy, directional changes and breaks of rhythm and balance. Without an obedient and responsive horse who will stop when asked, bend and turn instantly and willingly from the leg, the rider will stand no chance.

Some horses show more natural aptitude towards dressage than others, and regrettably I always seem to disadvantage myself by selecting horses primarily on their extreme suitability for galloping fast, jumping athletically and possessing stamina, rather than on any blatant dressage prowess. Even now, armed with hindsight and experience, I would still continue to pursue this policy, preferring not to sacrifice these attributes in favour of the qualities more readily found, for example, in a big-moving, highly receptive and settled warmblood horse.

So when it comes to dressage I have to try to make the most of what I've got. I therefore endeavour to perfect each horse's good points and minimise his bad ones in a systematic and sympathetic way in order to produce the best results possible. This is not always as easy as it sounds and one has to appreciate that in most event horses many of their fundamental problems arise from defects in conformation or temperament rather than from unwillingness. In coming to terms with this idea I have learnt patience.

I have also learned that it is pointless to resort to force in an effort to achieve instant success or short-term goals. This only serves to

At novice level the outline will be longer and lower but showing roundness and with an acceptance of the rider's hand. This horse is moving straight with an even contact on both reins.

As the horse attains a higher level of training he will be required to demonstrate more engagement and lightness, whilst retaining a rounded outline. Ricochet performing an extended trot at Badminton, 1993.

create underlying tension and mistrust. Because horses have no powers of reason it is always preferable to educate them by constant reward for work well done and quiet and consistent correction of mistakes.

Regardless of the level at which a rider is hoping to compete, the same basic principles should apply throughout the horse's training and performance, i.e. forward movement, rhythm and balance, suppleness combined with straightness, and relaxation and obedience. If these basic principles are instilled at novice level they can be developed further through to intermediate and refined for advanced work.

For example, at novice level the forward movement will be shown in a slightly freer fashion, with the horse in a round but longer and lower frame; there will be just an initial engagement of the hindquarters and a soft acceptance of the rider's hand, the horse thereby showing submission of the poll and jaw. But as the horse progresses he will be required to show increased engagement of the hocks, resulting in a greater collection of energy and a rounder

By teaching the horse to bend around the inside leg, it becomes possible to maintain a balanced forward rhythm while turning. The rider should look in the direction of travel and his shoulders should be in line with those of his horse.

outline. He will become more impulsive but should still work forwards into a soft acceptance of the bridle and ultimately into self-carriage, allowing him to cope more easily with the increased difficulty of lateral movements and counter-canter such as are required in advanced tests. The more collected the horse becomes, the lighter he should be in front; and it must be remembered to try and maintain the poll as the highest point to ensure that the horse does not become over-bent.

Rhythm and balance must be established at an early stage in the training, both within a pace and through transitions, during which the horse must remain constant in his outline. Again, some horses are much more naturally balanced than others due to their athleticism, conformation or degree of maturity.

By teaching the horse to bend his body when performing circles and negotiating corners, balance and rhythm will be maintained whilst still moving positively forward. Using the inside hand to slightly guide the horse, and the outside leg, supporting and placed well back to prevent the quarters from swinging out, the rider can increase the intensity of the inside leg on the girth to create flexion throughout the horse's body. This will cause the horse to bend or prescribe the arc of the turn or circle being executed. This must be possible whether going left or right, to ensure an equality of suppleness. Often, loss of rhythm and balance are noticeable when riders back off with the legs and slow down when approaching a corner. Throughout my horses' education I try to ride them (except when on straight lines) between my inside leg and outside hand, ensuring that when turning, their weight is driven from the inside hind leg well up into the outside shoulder, thus preventing them from falling in on the circles by placing their weight on the inside shoulder. Not only does this serve to assist the eventual progression into the lateral movements such as shoulder-in and half-pass, but it also helps greatly when negotiating, say, an excessively tight turn into a big, wide, oxer fence on a cross-country course when a balanced but forward approach is vital.

This is why I will introduce my horses to the exercise of leg-yielding very early on in their training. Usually I perform this movement from one straight line to another, and for ease use a dressage arena to assist me in the manoeuvre. For example, when riding on the outside track of the arena and after passing either A or C, I turn before the corner and ride straight down an imaginary quarter-line running five metres in from the track. From this line I endeavour to

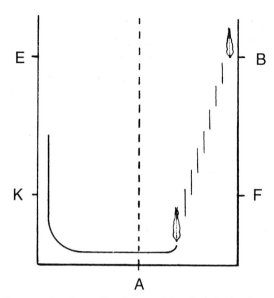

E   B

K   F

A

Leg-yielding from one line to another is a useful early introduction to lateral work, which encourages manoeuvrability and suppleness while establishing the horse's balance securely into the rider's outside hand. After passing A, I turn onto an imaginary quarter-line, midway between the centre line and the outside track. By allowing just a small bend at the horse's poll but otherwise keeping his body straight (i.e. parallel to the track) and more actively applying the inside leg at the girth, the horse is invited to 'yield' away from the leg, thereby travelling sideways and forward until reaching the track.

encourage the horse to move outwards towards the wall and away from the increased application of the inside leg, whilst still moving quietly forward. Hopefully, by keeping the horse's body straight and parallel to the long side of the arena but with just a slight bend at the poll away from the direction of the movement, the horse will soon respond by moving diagonally between the two lines, eventually reaching the wall. Sometimes at this point I will execute a ten-metre circle, so teaching the horse to stay off the inside leg and into the outside hand whilst keeping his bend to the inside of the circle.

It must be remembered that the objective of the exercise is for the horse to yield from the leg and therefore it is important that the inside hand does not cross over the neck, thereby producing a neck-reining effect. The inside hand should be offered slightly forward to allow the horse the freedom to cross over his forearm; it should not restrict as this would cause the steps to shorten or slow down, indicating a loss of impulsion. I believe it is essential that my horses completely understand that when I apply both legs they should move positively forward but when I apply only one leg then they should move away from that leg.

Straightness can only be achieved through an equality of feel in both hands. It is quite staggering how many horses, for various reasons, are heavier on one rein than the other. In many cases the rider can be blamed for creating this unevenness, by being one-sided himself. Often, though, riders do not attempt to correct the source of the problem in the preliminary stages and eventually are content to do a 'cover-up' job once they are working on more advanced movements.

Once the horse has become engaged and is moving up the levels he will be required to demonstrate variations in length of stride within the pace, at walk, trot and canter. Quite frequently with a young horse I will introduce medium work soon after any sideways movements, such as leg-yielding, to re-instil into his mind the desire to move forward. Again, there should be no loss of rhythm or balance.

It can be very tempting for a rider to push a horse out of his rhythm when trying to ride medium and extended paces in the hope of achieving bigger steps. My preparation for medium work is simply to try to create plenty of energy, riding the 'engine' up into a restraining hand, and then I offer the hand forward, allowing the horse to lengthen his frame and stride. When I want to make a downward transition back into a more collected stride I move the hand back again, taking up more contact, and ride the hindquarters underneath the horse, again maintaining the forward rhythm.

Varying the length of stride within a pace can be a useful tool for gauging straightness in a horse: if a horse will not take both hands forward evenly whilst still accepting a contact, he will show irregular or uneven steps and possibly crookedness as well.

Despite trying to follow the same basic principles when training my horses, I do not lose sight of the fact that each animal is an individual and will need fine tuning according to his own requirements. Messiah, for example, delights in jumping and galloping and finds the discipline needed for dressage exceedingly tedious. Although his good conformation and big, energetic forward movement allow him to perform the exercises easily, it is more important to ride Messiah's mind with care. Tension is his single biggest problem, and it usually arises through anticipation of more exciting things to come. If the dressage arenas at a competition are placed in view of the cross-country course then my task is almost always made more difficult.

At home I usually make his schooling simple to avoid confronta-

A useful way to relax a tense horse is to encourage him to take the contact forwards and down, working in a long and low frame. I also like to begin each schooling session in this fashion to ensure that the horse is swinging through from behind in an unrestricted manner. Many riders try to condense their horse's outline before free, forward movement has been established. In this photo the horse is starting to take the hand forward but could still stretch further down, with the nose a little more in advance of the poll.

tion and tend to work only on two or three specific movements during any one session. Always I start out long and low to get him completely relaxed, and I find this also to be a useful tactic for defusing him in a competition atmosphere. I then take up canter, rather than insist on any great collection in trot, as this prevents him from resisting the hand. The aim here is to get him moving through from behind. When I do start to ask him to round I find lateral work such as leg-yield and shoulder-in, and even pirouettes in walk, to be helpful. This strategy is designed to coerce him into shortening his frame without him realising it. If I were to trot him endlessly in large circles, fiddling with his mouth in the hope of putting him on the bit, I would simply end up with a tug-of-war on my hands.

Once Messiah is well connected and soft, the quality of his work can be quite outstanding - but, as was illustrated in Barcelona, the potential to explode is always there. I therefore try to positively emphasise in very black-and-white terms, the difference between good and bad. If his head comes up, hollowing his outline, he is told 'no' with a closing of my hands and legs; if he rounds he is told 'yes' by a softening of the hands. I have discovered that it is far easier to ride an excitable horse forward if he is in a round shape.

Shoulder-in can improve balance and control while encouraging suppleness.
(Below left) Here the horse is working correctly on three tracks, bent around the inside leg and secure in the outside rein. By applying an outside leg aid the horse could easily move from this shoulder-in into half-pass.
(Below right) In this photo the horse is moving incorrectly on four tracks and has tilted his nose. His body is too straight and he is not secure in the outside rein.

In contrast, Delta has a very good attitude, a receptive brain and always tries hard to please. She has trotting blood in her pedigree, which I guess contributes to her moving wide behind, especially in the medium and extended paces, and also to her four-time canter, most noticeable at a slower and more collected pace. Because of her naturally lower head carriage and her big hindquarters she tends to find it difficult to stay in balance when in a collected frame. To overcome this she is lunged a lot in side-reins before she begins her schooling, and this not only helps to relax her but also encourages her to find her own way forward into a balanced contact without the pressure from a rider. Because of her wide action behind and the power coming from her hindquarters I have to be careful not to let her run downhill. I have to work constantly at keeping her weight off her forehand, frequently slowing the rhythm down rather than pushing. Canter is her weakest pace and she must be kept coming forward on a rounder stride to prevent her breaking into a four-beat canter. Riding a lot of changes within a pace can help, in particular moving from working into medium and back, especially on a circle. Counter-canter is also useful, as long as I do not allow her to become too stilted.

Ricochet is similar to Messiah in that he would much prefer to be galloping and jumping, but 'Ric' is just a little less aggressive about it. He is typical of a horse who has come to eventing via a career in racing, but equally is testament to the fact that it is possible to retrain some former racehorses with a bit of extra effort. Even now, though, I suspect that his major problems are directly attributable to his racing experiences. He is very difficult to get off the left rein, particularly when galloping, and I imagine that this stems from his training in New Zealand, where all galloping takes place on circular tracks, and I suspect that he always went left-handed. He can also be somewhat difficult to keep 'on the aids' and tends to run through the bridle, thereby always being slightly ahead of me and lacking a little in control. This has been rectified to a certain extent by the constant use of half-halts. These are achieved by applying the seat and leg aids firmly, just slightly before checking with the reins, so momentarily steadying the horse's forward movement or pace. This 'checking' must, however, be followed immediately by a softening of the hand to allow the horse to move forward on a light contact. This process sometimes needs to be repeated several times in succession before Ricochet will stay light and in balance and not be inclined to rush off. Half-halt aids can be refined to the extent that

*FACING PAGE
Ricochet, a study of concentration, in full flight during the British Open Championships at Gatcombe Park, 1990.*

they can be applied throughout a dressage test not only to establish balance but also to attract the horse's attention to warn him that a stronger command might follow; and they can be executed without interrupting the rhythm of the pace.

FACING PAGE

(Top) Showing good technique over a wide oxer, Delta is beginning to turn in mid-air for a quick getaway. Brigstock, 1992.

(Bottom left) Delta hugging the rails on the steeplechase course at Badminton, 1993.

(Bottom right) Sitting back on Messiah to remain in balance over a drop fence. I am keeping the weight well off the horse's back and into the stirrups, at the same time slipping the reins to allow the horse sufficient freedom.

5

Three, Two, One ... *Go!*

————————— • —————————

WHEN cross-country schooling, probably the single most important factor in my mind is to ensure that I am building my horses' trust in me as their rider. At the same time I am looking to develop the horses' confidence in themselves.

Throughout my training I am careful never to overface an animal, but prefer a horse's education to be completely progressive and unhurried. Over the years I have learnt that it is wiser to be safe than sorry, as even the slightest scare can cause long-term damage to a horse's confidence, and also that of his rider.

It is never too early to begin cross-country schooling provided the horse is already capable of negotiating straightforward show jumps and simple logs and rails. There really is no substitute for experience gained through putting 'miles on the clock'. Horses need to be taught about cross-country obstacles before they start competing, so I take beginners to schooling sessions where I can introduce them to the type of problems they are likely to encounter. At this point I am careful only to ask simple questions over fences of the smallest dimensions.

Sometimes I will make sure that a 'baby' is escorted by an older, more experienced horse, at least for the first few sessions. If he runs into an 'anxiety attack', say, when first meeting a ditch or water fence, then encouragement can be given by way of company or a lead.

In the early stages, little and often (small doses administered frequently) is the desired treatment. Constructive repetition over a variety of different obstacles early on will help to cement a partnership and build an understanding between horse and rider. A solid

FACING PAGE
Showing good form over a wide oxer and ditch at Saumur, 1992, with Delta.

A steady, progressive early education is essential. Here a young horse is being gently introduced to the 'horrors' of water in an unhurried manner. I find nervous youngsters can be encouraged by the company of older, more experienced horses, who can offer the novice a lead if necessary.

foundation must be laid before moving on to more demanding problems.

I very rarely school my advanced horses over fences that exceed novice dimensions, for fear of unnecessarily risking or scaring even the seasoned campaigners. I prefer to continue improving technique, athleticism, accuracy and obedience over an assortment of small obstacles, ensuring that once I do arrive at competitions the horses are bursting with confidence and know-how. The added lift from the sense of occasion and atmosphere, combined with the flow of being 'on course', will help you achieve any extra height over the bigger fences.

Usually the more experienced the horse that I'm riding, the less likely I am to want to go cross-country schooling between competitions, although I would want to sort out any problems or areas of weakness. To be honest I prefer a horse who shows an aversion to a single type of fence (as was initially the case with Messiah and water jumps) to one who chose to stop at random. In the case of the former, at least I can single out the problem fence for special treatment. I believe that an intelligent rider can work on a horse's 'phobia' and school it out of him with patient and constructive practice.

I can still vividly recall my own dislike of corner jumps, which probably stemmed from not understanding how to maintain an accurate line and balanced approach. There was a time when I would avoid attempting a corner at all costs, and at novice level this is normally possible as alternative routes are offered. However, once I upgraded to intermediate and advanced I was confronted with corner fences with no options, and my dilemma increased in direct

'Perhaps', a young novice horse participating at his first competition. He is showing outstanding technique but, through lack of experience, is overly suspicious of the fence.

In my early career I had a phobia about corner fences. In order to overcome this problem I had to go back to grass-roots level and practise until my confidence grew. Here I am taking a young horse over the direct route at a novice corner, teaching us both that there is nothing to fear.

proportion to the size and angle of fence. It took some time to work out that without a solid foundation of confidence gained over small corner fences, the larger ones were not going to get any easier. I had to go right back to the beginning. By frequently practising over simple corner fences constructed of show-jump poles and barrels, I was able to learn to develop a correct, controlled canter on the approach and train my horses to stay straight. Later I moved on to small fixed corners and began negotiating these fences in competitions, even if an alternative was offered. Thankfully I now feel confident enough to tackle even the most difficult corners, such as the Vicarage Vee at Badminton, comfortable in the knowledge that the groundwork has been successfully completed.

I now apply the same basic principle to all my cross-country training and ensure that I understand the correct technique and approach required to negotiate each type of fence in balance and therefore with confidence.

To help me judge what is necessary for each obstacle, I try to grade the different fences on a imaginary scale. At one end of the scale might be, say, a bounce of upright rails with a downhill approach, and at the opposite end a nine-foot wide ditch with a bullfinch brush behind. Somewhere in the middle of this scale come all the **straightforward fences**, such as logs, hay bales, hedges and the like, that can be taken with as little fuss and bother as possible. These 'easier' fences should be used to give the horse a comfortable, enjoyable experience and should serve to bolster his confidence even further. No time should be wasted in checking the pace or setting up the distance for take-off. They should be jumped out of the existing stride without any break in rhythm. This will only be possible, though, if the horse is already galloping in a good shape with a rounded stride, and is well up together between the rider's leg and hand. I do not look too hard for a pre-determined take-off spot for if the horse is sufficiently engaged and moving forward in control, a suitable take-off point will appear. Obviously with experience the rider's eye becomes better tuned to assess the distance and the rider is able to influence the stride, but essentially I believe that it is more valuable to encourage the horse to look and think for himself over these 'user-friendly' obstacles, thereby sharpening his awareness and self-preservation.

A good **cross-country time** will be better achieved by moving forward with control and simply jumping these straightforward fences out of the horse's stride, than by galloping wildly around the course only to have to haul the horse up in front of each obstacle to restore sufficient balance to jump. If just one second is wasted in this manner, trying to set the horse up for each fence, then the cumulative effect of this time-wasting over a whole course can dramatically affect a rider's overall time; moreover it is disruptive to the flow. Nor do we particularly want the horse to bascule high and round over simple, straightforward fences because, again, precious seconds will be ticking away. Unlike in show jumping, a slightly flatter, broad arc through the air and a quick get-away begin to become essential.

For all remaining obstacles that tend towards a more **vertical** nature, thereby offering a less friendly profile, I prefer to keep a slightly more rounded, controlled stride on the approach, and sometimes a reduction in pace will be needed. I allow the obstacle to

A spread fence should be met on a lengthening stride to ensure that there is sufficient scope and impulsion to negotiate the width easily. Delta's excellent jumping style over this imposing table shows that the approach must have been correct.

'come up to me', waiting for the fence instead of pushing towards it. However, when doing this it can be very easy to forget to keep the engine running (i.e. the back end engaged) sufficiently to avoid a stop. To overcome this it is worthwhile remembering to collect the stride by riding with the leg, pushing the back end of the horse up into a restraining hand, rather than by pulling the front of the horse backwards. This again will help to keep the forward movement and assist in maintaining a quicker time.

For fences that involve a **spread**, the stride will no longer remain collected but will need to extend or lengthen to enable the horse to have enough scope to clear the width of the fence with ease. An onlooker should not be able to discern a noticeable or obvious difference in the stride pattern, such should be the subtlety of the adjustment - and, again, the rhythm should not be broken throughout the whole course.

The necessary speed should always be directly related to the type of problem presented. Large, inviting and solid, imposing fences can be tackled with perhaps a little more pace than intricate upright combinations.

With practice, rider and horse can learn the correct techniques to handle themselves well over the varied fences that make up most courses - fences such as banks, steps, drops, sunken roads, water, ditches, corners and combinations - as well as the more modern tests of accuracy and obedience such as arrowheads and angles. Familiarity will assist, of course, coupled with progressive training, particularly when learning to cope with ditches, often the downfall of many hopeful partnerships.

I would definitely place **ditches** in the category of spread fences because some can be seriously wide. It is important not to look down into the bottom of a ditch, but to set your sights well beyond it on the landing side. The same theory needs to be applied to the horse, by which I mean that you should keep his head up and not allow him to peer down into the depths by kind permission of a loosened rein contact.

During early training (or re-training), I introduce the horse to the smallest of ditches without hurrying, and once he is confidently popping back and forth without hesitation, I begin to instil the correct technique into his mind. The approach should be as for any other spread: a slightly increasing length of stride and impulsion. Sometimes it helps to imagine that the ditch has a triple bar built over the top of it.

All too often, though, the complete opposite happens on the approach - the horse shortens his stride and there is a decrease in energy and loss of impulsion - with the result that the horse cat-leaps or refuses. Thus it may be useful when teaching horses about ditches to reinforce the rider's leg with the use of the whip. To confirm the horse's forward-thinking attitude, a short but effective tap of the whip directly behind the leg, right on the point of take-off, will do wonders to reassure a tentative participant. I would never hit a horse on the shoulder as this tends to distract his attention and

When negotiating ditch fences it is important not to peer down into the depths of the ditch, but instead to look up and ahead for dry land! The horse's head should also be kept up so he will not be unduly bothered by what lies below ground level. Like all spread fences, ditches should be met on a lengthening stride.

reassures only the rider who cannot remove his hand from the rein efficiently. When the lesson has been successfully learnt, the whip can be stored away and need only be reapplied if and when the lengthening approach fails and indecision appears. Once a horse has learnt to lengthen positively towards a ditch, without fear, then he is unlikely to be troubled by whatever variation a course designer chooses to construct.

Likewise, **water** should be introduced slowly to green horses. If time is spent in educating a horse early in its career, the benefits will be reaped later on. I would not start off by asking a horse to jump straight into water but would find a gentle approach that would allow him to walk and trot in easily. Once in the water it can be wise to stay in and not let the horse rush out immediately on the opposite side. This was a problem with Messiah, in his early days. He would leap extravagantly into water, through a desire to please, but terrified by his fear of water he would bolt out as quickly as he could. By walking around in the water for a few minutes every time he jumped in, he soon learned to relax and not be afraid.

When I introduce jumping in from a bank, I first approach in a slow trot then quietly build the momentum until the horse jumps out and down, landing securely rather than floundering in, one leg after the other. I do not want him to slow himself down excessively as he nears the edge. Later, when cantering, I try to maintain a short, bouncy stride, allowing the horse to assess the situation on the approach while still moving forward. Riding with too much speed

This unusual feat of agility from Ricochet at Blenheim demonstrates why water fences should not be taken with too much speed. Controlled impulsion has allowed him to negotiate the vertical poles on entry yet given him time to appreciate the impending water. It has been necessary to keep my weight back to avoid being caught ahead of the movement.

can cause the horse to back off or become nervous - or even to fall on landing. When horses jump into water with pace, the sudden drag of water on the horse's legs (if any depth or drop in is significant) creates a dramatic check on the forward movement.

When jumping over an obstacle into water, again the approach should be made with a collected but active canter. Whilst the speed is reduced the impulsion should not be, as although the water will influence the approach foremost, the obstacle needs to be cleared before worrying about the landing. Fences that do not incorporate drops into water can be ridden with a bit more positive pace.

A fence placed on a **uphill slope** almost always seems to ride more easily than a similar one on a downhill approach. I guess this is because on the uphill incline the weight and balance is likely to be more naturally distributed over the hindquarters, the source of the jumping effort. Usually the steeper the slope, the stronger and more impulsive the rider can be.

When going **downhill** it becomes considerably more difficult to ensure that the back end is engaged and that the weight is sufficiently off the forehand. To start with, it would be wise to trot into this type of fence, not jumping anything too high or too upright until balance can be established. As mentioned earlier, when giving lessons I always suggest that my pupils sit up but don't sit down. This will teach them to use the legs to generate the balance rather than removing the legs and relying on the seat too much. The horse needs the freedom to bring his hocks underneath him and does not want to be hampered by a rider heavily slumped on his back. By sitting up, the shoulders should not get ahead of the centre of balance and the security will remain down into the heel.

Banks and **steps up** are obstacles where the rider will be able to get well forward, and because of the physical effort involved the approach will need to be energetic and impulsive. However, the stride must not be allowed to become strung-out or the horse may not be able to spring high enough to allow his landing gear to put down on the higher level. Again, the rider's eyes should remain focused up and ahead and the seat should remain out of the saddle with the weight taken on the stirrup.

A **coffin** or **sunken road**, like a water jump, should be taken off a short but powerful stride. Too much speed could result in the horse experiencing an element of surprise when he suddenly sights the ditch or falling ground beyond. The more upright the fence into the complex, the bouncier the stride will need to be, and again maxi-

Steps up, like banks, require great physical effort and therefore should be taken with maximum impulsion. However, the stride should not be allowed to get too long but should be kept reasonably collected to create enough spring. The energy level should not be allowed to die on the way up, whether or not there is another fence to be negotiated at the top.

mum amounts of controlled revs will be required if a refusal is to be avoided. These types of fence are usually best approached dead straight as they can be unforgiving if the horse, jumping on an angle, becomes slightly uneven with his front feet. A rub can sometimes produce a twisting that can unseat the rider. Once down into a sunken road or over the ditch element of a coffin, it is important to

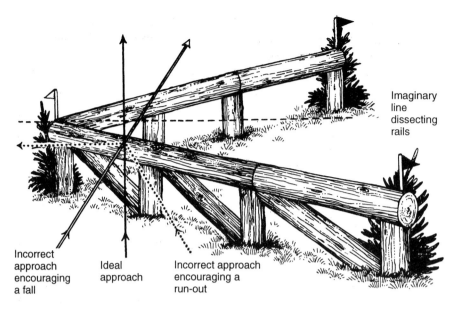

To avoid a mishap when negotiating a simple corner (as above), it is necessary to make a controlled and accurate approach, maintaining a straight course. I would normally dissect the angle of the two rails with an imaginary line and aim to come in on a line perpendicular to this, thereby reducing the chances of a run-out or fall.

maintain the impulsion so that sufficient energy is generated to negotiate the exit, which will be on rising or higher ground.

Fences that require a jump from **light into dark** or a landing into the unknown should be jumped in the same manner as a coffin. Time must be allowed in the approach for the horse's eyes to adjust or for him to evaluate the problem, eliminating the element of surprise.

As mentioned previously, **corners** are a test of accuracy and control. First the rider must know where he intends to aim and then he must hold that line. It is not normally possible to be exactly perpendicular to the front rail as inevitably that would result in the possibility of landing on the back rail. Likewise aiming straight at the back rail will result in offering the horse the option of running out. So the angle of the two problems should be dissected by an imaginary line and it is at this dissection of the two rails that I aim (see diagram above).

It can sometimes be necessary to walk the exact line several times to be sure of getting it right, and if possible it can be useful to sight up the correct line with a fixed object of distinction well ahead in the distance. If I were ever to consider deviating off the ideal approach then I would tend to jump slightly more from the outside towards the inner part of the fence, trusting my horse's scope a little and blocking out the open space to the outside of the flag. However, this is not very often necessary as usually I know that the horse I am riding can be trusted to stay straight as a result of much schooling. The stride should be reasonably short to ensure accuracy - the longer the stride, the less influence the rider will have. There needs to be plenty of impulsion as unless you are clever enough to jump right over the edge of the corner then the fence will indeed incorporate a spread.

There are many exercises that can be used to develop accurate riding in preparation for jumping corners, arrowheads and angled or narrow fences. I practise frequently at home using just basic materials. For example, a single coloured show-jump fence can be utilised in many ways. I may choose first to approach straight but will see if I can hold a line directly over a selected section of paintwork, not necessarily always the centre stripe. Then I might approach from left to right, angling the same fence and still jumping directly over the designated spot. Right to left should be practised too, to ensure equal efficiency on both sides. The same simple fence set diagonally on the centre line of an arena will present yet another challenge.

Jumping an **arrowhead** or any fence that offers only a narrow panel at which to aim is simply another test of keeping the horse straight and maintaining accuracy. It is wise to practise these types of fence in moderation by constructing small replicas from rails and, say, barrels or sections of walls. To begin with, the problem can be easy with encouraging wings to teach the horse to stay on course. By gradually reducing or narrowing the front panel the horse should still remain straight, but trust and understanding between horse and rider should increase. Once I have the correct response from my horses at such obstacles I don't go on repeating the exercise to the point of actually asking for trouble - in the form of a run-out - to occur. Instead I go back to my idea of maintaining the correct line over a specific spot on a show jump or even on a certain post on a cross-country fence, rather than too many open-sided, narrow panels.

Drop jumps need to be learnt to be negotiated but they are not a fence that I tend to practise a lot as they can be a little too punishing on the horse's legs. Too much drop-jumping is more likely to make a horse cautious rather than brave. If an obstacle is to be cleared at the edge of the drop then a controlled and balanced approach with not

Jumps can't be negotiated perfectly every time, and stickability can sometimes save the day. This sequence shows an awkward moment for Delta at the Badminton Quarry in 1993, and whilst we didn't win any points for copybook style, we were nevertheless able to continue unpenalised.

...Having survived, it is important to recover concentration quickly to prepare for the next fence, which in this case happened to be three strides away.

too much speed will be required to avoid buckling over on landing. I like to get my horses together in sufficient time before the fence so that I am able to ride a little more forward in the last few strides. This way the horses tend to jump more smoothly out with a less steep descent and therefore land more securely with their weight behind their front legs - not in front. This will also help to make them easier to sit on when landing. There is much debate as to whether it is wisest to sit back over drops. I personally prefer to do this unless the ground runs away sharply on landing, in which case the forward movement will probably hardly alter, as the force of gravity and the slope of the gradient will ensure that the horse keeps on going. Dropping down onto flat ground, however, normally means that the horse will slow considerably and it is therefore undesirable to get ahead of the centre of balance. By opening out the upper body, and folding back from the hips, the rider will still be able to absorb the impact of landing on the stirrup and will be in a defensive position should a stumble occur. By slipping the reins through slightly opened fingers, the horse will be given sufficient freedom without the contact being completely lost. On touch-down

Fences involving a substantial drop down onto level ground demand that the rider adapts his position to remain in balance. The shoulders should move back and the reins must slip through the hands to prevent the rider from being pitched forwards as the horse lands and the momentum is checked. An increased length of stride will encourage the horse to jump out, lessening the angle of descent. Ricochet at Thirlestane Castle, 1992, where he won the Scottish Open.

the fingers can close on the reins and immediately begin to gather them up again in the first stride forward.

There is little doubt that cross-country schooling and competing is a high-risk sport, so paramount importance must be placed upon safety. I never try to run before I can walk. If I don't feel I can maintain a balanced approach in gallop then I will canter, or if still not confidently controlled, I will trot. It is worth remembering that you should only go as fast across country as you safely can. However, if the correct training is completed and a solid foundation of balance and control is laid early on then eventually your speed across country can in fact be quite rapid.

6

OVER THE POLES

——————— • ———————

As DISCUSSED earlier in the chapter on rider technique, I believe a common theme should run consistently through the three phases of competition and be present in all the attendant training. But more riders abandon sound riding principles when show jumping than in any other phase, the common theme being swept by the board. For example, a rider may successfully negotiate an excellent cross-country round on one day, by using a strong leg and light seat into a controlling hand, then suddenly change his riding style completely the next day when entering the show-jumping arena, just because coloured poles have a reputation for falling. Without warning, he will immediately adopt defensive tactics - by sitting up and starting to pull on the reins - forgetting completely about the importance of the basic principles that helped him to succeed in the earlier dressage and cross-country stages.

In the show jumping it is still important that the rider strives to ride forward; but now the control, the length of stride and the energy level all need to be slightly refined.

I have also talked earlier about the importance of sitting still with an independent seat, but disregarding actual position, we must have an understanding of what we are trying to achieve. Instead of adopting new techniques, we must still try to maintain all that is necessary to produce a dressage test and all that is necessary to negotiate a cross-country course successfully. We are still wanting rhythm - in this case from the start flags right through to the finish, flowing forward in a balanced and controlled manner. We still need to be prepared for each fence, just as we need to be prepared for each movement in the dressage arena, or for each fence on the cross-

country. I am astonished by the number of riders I see trying to negotiate a turn on the approach to a show jump whilst on the wrong lead. How can they expect to clear the fence successfully? They can't. They can only hope, as they are certainly not enhancing their chances by being so unbalanced.

If I found myself in this situation, I would immediately attempt a flying change as all my horses are taught how to do this manoeuvre. But if my horse didn't know how to do flying changes and I had landed on the wrong leg, I would immediately trot a few steps, take up the correct canter lead and thus be well prepared for the next fence.

The less complicated we can make our show-jumping technique, the less chance we have of making mistakes. I try to maintain a very simple way of going and if my horse waivers to either side of the desired 'norm', I will make an adjustment to bring him back into line.

Much can be done at home to improve a horse's technique and also, for that matter, a rider's. Sometimes, though, it is the psychological effects of the show-jumping phase that have the most bearing on a rider's performance. To overcome this I would recommend frequent practice at show-jumping competitions. It is all too easy to specialise solely in eventing, and not clock up enough mileage in show-jumping arenas to become both relaxed and confident about what you are doing. A rider like myself, who competes on several horses, is immediately advantaged because of the number of sorties that I make in a season; so one-horse riders really do need to spend time honing their skills in show-jumping classes in between their horse trials competitions.

At home I tend to concentrate mainly on gymnastic-type exercises that will improve the suppleness, athleticism, balance and awareness of the horse, but I am careful not to overtax the horse physically. Quite often these exercises are performed in trot, simply testing the horse's manoeuvrability and control. When I do canter into fences at home I try consistently to arrive 'deep' on take-off: that is to say, I don't over-protect the horse, but instead ride positively forward to the bottom of the fence. This way he should learn to back off from the fence of his own accord and become instinctively careful, focusing his attention on the job in hand. Instead of looking hard for the ideal take-off spot, and thereby possibly holding the horse off the fence, I simply keep coming in a good canter rhythm. If the stride is sufficiently round, then I'm unlikely to miss my desired take-off

FACING PAGE
By offering a crest release along the horse's neck, it is possible for the rider to keep the weight down into the heel and remain in balance rather than toppling forward. It also allows the horse to lower the head and neck, enabling the shoulder and forearm to lift. It is not possible for a horse to make a good bascule if the head remains high.

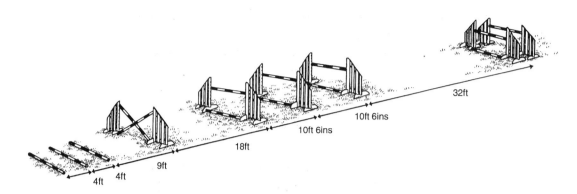

This example of a gymnastic grid will improve the athleticism and elasticity of the horse while testing the rider's balance and effectiveness. The approach should be made in trot with the pace well controlled. The double bounce will serve both to shorten the horse's frame and to sharpen his technique. This, in turn, may cause a loss of forward energy, which the rider must maintain to cover successfully the two long strides to the remaining oxer. A heavy, driving seat will only interfere with the horse's efforts and create a hollow and hurried reaction.

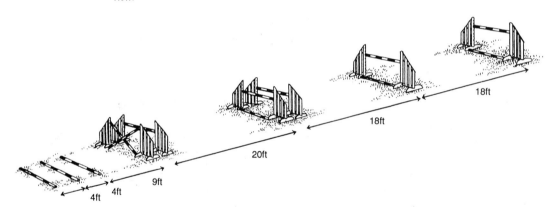

Different challenges can be devised by redesigning the sequence of fences incorporated in grid exercises. Here an immediate high level of energy will be required to negotiate easily from trot the two oxers at the beginning. Thereafter, with the reducing length of the remaining strides, the horse should be encouraged to steady and shorten. It will be necessary for the rider to sit up a little and remain secure over the centre of the horse's balance to allow his mount the opportunity to 'back off' the later obstacles. If the rider pushes his shoulders forward at each fence he will only encourage the horse to become long and flat and will risk getting ahead of the movement.

point. Anyhow, it's only when the horse is insufficiently engaged, or the rider is over-emphasising the point of take-off, that things seem to go terribly wrong.

Once in the ring, especially on the last day of a three-day event when the horse may be tired, this is the time to start thinking about helping the horse, perhaps by holding him together a little more and daring him a little less. But while schooling I tend always to put the onus on the horse and just ride forward with this in mind.

Most of the grids that I train my horses over tend to be built with reasonably short distances. This helps to teach the horse to back up and shorten his frame further. It is always much easier to kick-on and open up a bit when presented with a longer distance, than it is to try and shorten a horse that has been allowed to travel in a long, strung-out shape.

Mostly I start all my grids with trot poles evenly spaced on the ground. I usually set down about three of four, which will help to keep the rhythm and balance of the trot. If a horse shows a tendency to break from trot into canter when approaching a fence, then it is often inevitable that, without the rider realising it, the horse will break from canter to a kind of gallop. Instead he must learn to wait, keeping his hocks well underneath him and remaining in balance right up to the point of take-off.

When negotiating grids, the horse should remain straight and in the middle of each fence. The horse must learn that once he has entered a grid, the only way out is at the far end. Thus, when it comes to a competition, the horse's instinct will be to complete the fences in front of him, without distraction.

I normally make the first element of a grid a cross-pole, as this will help to guide the horse to the middle of the grid and encourage him to be immediately tight with his forelegs. A young horse may need this assistance to execute the first jump as he will be concentrating on what lies ahead. The remainder of the grid fences are constructed from a single raised pole with a ground rail at each fence. If the horse does make a mistake, he is less likely to injure himself if there are fewer poles on each fence.

Once I have entered a grid, I always insist that my horses leave only by the exit at the other end. A run-out is immediately corrected. If the horse has gone to the right, I bring him back into the left; and likewise, if he goes to the left, he must be brought back to the right. Thus he learns that he must stay straight and that he must keep going as there is only one exit down at the far end. Again, I would endeavour not to overface a green horse and would only increase the heights and difficulty if I felt he was confident.

Although I have given two examples of grid exercises on page 70, there is no limit to the variety of sequences that you can construct to encourage the horse to jump in an effective and athletic manner. You can alter the distance between two fences to make it one stride or two, or even three, and the more you are able to change the layout of the grid, the more you will encourage your horse to think for himself.

One thing that I don't like to practise over too frequently are series of bounce fences. Although bounces can serve to sharpen the horse's reactions and make him shorten his frame, unless they are built reasonably high, they tend to encourage a horse to spend very little time in the air. They seem to make horses anxious to put their front feet down to land, almost before their back legs have left the ground, possibly in readiness for the next effort. So I tend to keep my bounce-jumping to a minimum.

When not actually jumping grids, the remainder of my work tends to centre around the way in which the horses travel between the fences. I spend much time working on balance and rhythm, on related lines (shortening and lengthening the stride), turning into fences and gaining control.

Even if you have just two fences, much good work can be done. For example, at home I might build a simple oxer and a straightforward vertical with a ground rail on each side of the fences. These two fences can be jumped in both directions, off both reins, in sequence, or in a variety of separate ways. If I set them, say, six regu-

Exercises for related distances. *Two fences - one an upright, the other an oxer - are set up 80 feet, i.e. six average strides, apart.*

Jumping left to right with six strides: establish correct rhythm and ensure that six strides are confidently possible. Keep the stride pattern regular.

Jumping right to left (which will help prevent anticipation) with seven strides: reduce the energy level (slow down) and close up the length of stride (coil the spring). The approach to the first fence must be reduced, and the first stride on landing must be immediately short so the rhythm is not disrupted. The seven strides must be even.

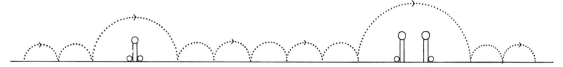

Jumping from left to right for five strides: the stride needs to be lengthened (uncoiling the spring). Allow the hand to go forward rather than kick on, to avoid the horse speeding up. Lengthen the stride on the approach to the first fence and ensure that the first stride on landing is forward. A light seat will prevent the horse from hollowing.

lar 12-foot non-jumping strides apart, I could ride the distance between them on a balanced, even six strides, and then, if I chose, I could reverse the direction and perhaps put in an additional stride to fit in seven more-rounded but still even strides. To do this I will require more control and more collection: I will need to reduce the energy level by bringing my shoulders and hands back, and thereby close up the length of the horse's stride in my approach to the first fence. On landing, I will keep this increased collection and add an extra stride before the second fence. Similarly, I may choose to come back again from the other direction, and this time ride forward with an offering hand and an increased length of stride, taking only five strides, still on the original distance.

Exercises such as these allow me to test my horse's athleticism, receptiveness and control (see diagrams above). Sometimes I will just jump the first fence, halt half-way between the fences and then walk away, as this prevents the horse anticipating and continuing straight to the next fence. When teaching, it's quite surprising to note how many of my pupils' horses literally take control and simply run on to the next fence, regardless of the rider's wishes.

Using these same two fences, I can also work on my turns. Riding on a short turn and turning back on myself to the vertical, I will simply maintain the balance, control and rhythm that I have already established, but when making the turn back on myself towards the oxer, I will need to increase the length of stride to ensure that I have sufficient energy to jump cleanly over the back rail.

I mentioned earlier the need to be able to execute flying lead changes, but even more efficient is the ability to dictate which leg the horse lands on. I always insist that my horses are 'ambidextrous' and do not show stiffness, landing on whichever leading leg I decide. To work on this, I might construct a small grid down the centre line of the arena, and off to the left, about four or five strides later, I will place a fence; off to the right, four or five strides later, I will place another fence. Starting out in trot over the grid, I will decide whether I want to go over the left-hand fence or the one on the right, and indicate this to the horse as he completes the grid. If I choose to go left, by slightly opening the left-hand rein and putting a little more weight into my left stirrup I will effectively tell the horse which way I intend to go. As he jumps the last part of the grid and

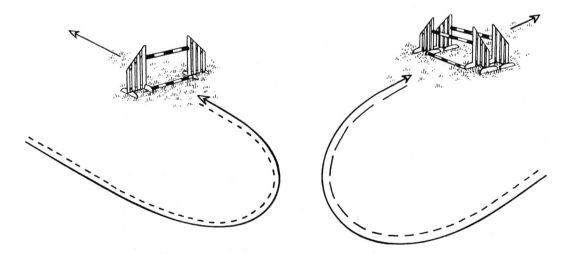

This exercise makes use of the two fences set up for the related distance work (see p.73). The fences can be approached off either leg. When turning, keep the eyes on the fence, and maintain the rhythm, balance and forward movement. You will need to keep the stride round (as for the seven-stride distance on p.73) as you approach the vertical; and lengthen the stride (as for the five-stride distance on p.73) when tackling the parallel.

It is important for a horse to be 'ambidextrous' to enable the rider to move between fences on either rein without interruption. Whilst actually in the air over a jump, the rider should look in the desired direction, place more weight onto the inside stirrup and lead slightly with the inside rein, to indicate to the horse which canter lead to take up on landing.

his legs are level, he will find it easy to come down with his left fore-leg moving forward and simply maintain left canter toward the left-hand jump. Likewise, it is important that he is able to do the same to the right when the appropriate signals are given. Consciously looking in the intended direction helps to place me in the position I want to be, in advance, and to give the necessary aids. Most horses will have a tendency to land on one leg or the other, so it is up to the rider to find out which leg his horse favours and ensure that he is equally supple.

By slightly varying the construction of a few fences, we can begin to improve the horse's jumping technique or strengthen any areas in which it may be weak. For example, if a horse is becoming a touch nervous about his jumping, I will roll the ground pole out an extra six or eight inches to help him sight his take-off point and back off the top rail, thereby giving him more time to think about (and execute) his jump.

If a horse was not worried about his jumping, but was too strong, rushing his fences and not backing off, I would construct an inverted vee shape using two extra poles in front of the fence (see photo

Strong horses who show little respect for their fences may find this exercise useful. The two poles arranged in an inverted vee in front of the fence create a narrowing take-off point, inviting the horse to slow down and pay more attention to the job in hand. The claustrophobic effect of the added poles will encourage the horse to back off the fence and gain more height. This arrangement will also assist in keeping the horse straight.

FACING PAGE
Putting it all into practice - Delta at Burghley, 1992. During training sessions the horse is encouraged to think for himself, but once in the ring, especially on the last day of a three-day event when the horse may be tired, the rider should offer him every assistance.

above). This will create a slightly claustrophobic channel for the horse, who will find himself running into a narrowing point. He will then be more likely to slow down, sit back on his hocks, and jump higher into the air, without the rider having to pull excessively on the reins. This device can also help in straightening a horse, but if a horse tended to drift to one side, for example to the left, I would rest a single pole just left of the centre of the fence, running down to the ground, to correct the problem.

If a horse showed consistent disregard by always knocking down the front rail of a parallel, I would place a pole diagonally from one front corner of the fence to the opposite back corner, lying it across the top of the two poles that make up the parallel. This would serve not only to make the rails more secure in the cups, but also to create an optical illusion that would encourage the horse to shift the highest point of his bascule more towards the front of his jump, thereby encouraging him to pay more respect to the front pole.

To improve the technique of a horse who repeatedly knocks

fences down with his back legs only, or one whose style is a bit cramped behind (i.e. he brings his legs up under his stomach instead of trailing them out behind), I would work him frequently over an oxer fence set up as follows: a fairly tall cross-pole in front, with a low bar out behind, say, six feet from the cross-pole. This would encourage him first to jump up into the air, then lower his head and kick up his back end more in the second half of his bascule. The height of the cross-pole and the claustrophobic effect that it too produces, will invite the horse to reach additional height behind and open out.

Similarly, a horse who tended to get over his shoulder, that is to say, one who pushes most of his bodyweight forward in front of his forelegs (as was the case with Messiah early on), would be mostly jumped over oxers, but low and wide and with the back bar slightly higher than the front. This encourages the horse to bring his forearm forward to complete the spread of the fence; and I especially like using combinations of oxers for this purpose.

With my young horses I like to make sure that they are well introduced to a variety of fences before they are ever likely to meet them in competition. If I can get access to, say, a brush jump, some planks, a gate, and a wall, I will make sure that the horse is confidently popping over these fences before he enters the ring.

Just as in the cross-country training, I will make sure that he starts first in trot, and builds his impulsion as he gets closer to the fence, perhaps breaking into canter in the last few strides. This way he will be better able to assess the problems presented by the fence on his approach and will build confidence as he gets closer. This is preferable to having him approaching at speed and decelerating in the last few strides to see what he has to do. Even now, I still have to jump Messiah backwards and forwards over small water trays, because he has always had an aversion to them. He tends to want to rush quickly across the top, but with steady, repetitive work his confidence grows.

All these exercises should help to improve performance and enable the rider to become more aware of the way a horse 'ticks' and operates. However, at the end of the day it is predominantly the horse who has to be careful over the jumps. Take Ricochet, for example: although he never show jumps quite as conventionally as I would like, he nevertheless has a genuine desire to leave the fences standing, and to date has completed all his international three-day events without dislodging a pole.

It is very difficult to make a careless horse careful, and whilst many event riders would reject, say, a horse that did not move well or one that lacked courage, I would reject one that did not possess a tidy show-jumping technique. There is just too much at stake on the last day of a competition to be let down by a poor performance in the jumping arena.

7

TOOLS OF THE $TRADE$

———————— • ————————

W HEN riding my horses at competitions I am constantly trying to minimise the amount of tack they wear, believing that good training is ultimately of more use than sophisticated paraphernalia.

Some may be surprised to discover that I try to ride exclusively in snaffle bits. In fact, I possess very little else. Basically if I cannot control a particular horse in a snaffle bit then I have no great desire to continue with it any further and would describe the animal as unsuitable. More often than not the problems of control lie within the horse's brain, not its mouth.

I cannot help but be amused by riders who fly at speed round novice cross-country courses, decked out in martingales, complicated bits and several reins. What a handful - and what on earth are these riders going to resort to when they eventually upgrade to intermediate, where they will be required not only to increase the pace but also to show more control? To my mind a careful education is needed to produce sensible, controlled balance, and this is a must before the addition of speed.

Once a horse reaches advanced level and is facing tougher competition, where the results become more important, it is more acceptable to use something other than a snaffle. Even so, if the training has been correct such a measure should be quite unnecessary. I am not suggesting here that a rider should be expected to approach, say, a vertical bounce of rails with a drop into a water complex without sufficient control to negotiate the obstacle. However, I have found that any lack of control that I have experienced in the past has been more attributable to having too much pace for the fence in question rather than to a lack of brakes. Perhaps when I get

FACING PAGE
Messiah taking the direct route onto the barn roof, heading for the first water complex. Barcelona Olympics, 1992.

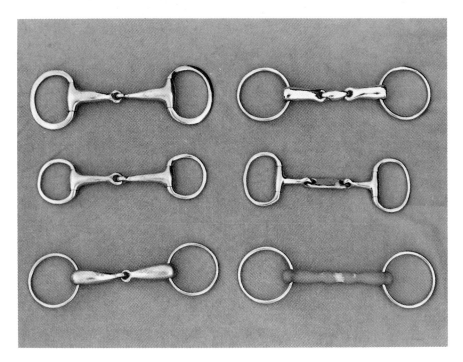

A selection of straightforward snaffle bits that I use on my horses. Left, top to bottom: a mild, thick eggbutt (for fussy-mouthed horses); a thin eggbutt (for strong horses); a loose-ringed, hollow-mouth (which I tend to favour most). Right, top to bottom: a KK training bit (to vary the pressure points - suits Tempo especially); a Dr Bristol (for over-enthusiasm on the cross-country); a straight-bar rubber snaffle (to encourage light-mouthed horses to accept a contact, e.g. Ra Ora).

totally submerged in a water jump one day soon I will alter my way of thinking.

I do, however, own a wide selection of snaffle bits. For dressage I mainly opt for a lightweight hollow-mouthed, loose-ring type, of reasonable thickness in order that the horse may be ridden onto a confident contact. Occasionally, with a fussy-mouthed horse I will use an eggbutt, or with a constantly strong horse, a thinner version. Sometimes, at the other extreme of the scale, I might use a rubber snaffle on a horse that has an exceptionally light mouth or one that is unwilling to take a proper contact, although I would hope to employ this only as a short-term measure.

Rarely when jumping do I change the bitting from that used in the dressage, although for the cross-country, on a horse whose enthusiasm is over-riding its manners, I may go for a stronger Dr Bristol or Waterford snaffle. I find it advisable to alternate bits from time to time so that the horses do not become too fixed or heavy on any particular one.

FACING PAGE

(Top left) Ricochet making a splash at the Lake, Badminton, 1993.

(Top right) Sitting tight at the Dog Kennels. Messiah, en route to the World Championship title at Stockholm, 1990.

(Bottom) Adopting a defensive position: the heel is well down, the leg is braced forward, the shoulders are up and I am keeping a good contact. Delta jumping with speed and enthusiasm - Belton, 1993.

I prefer to use rubber-gripped reins as, besides being non-slip, they offer a firm feel in the hand, look good and are extremely strong. They maintain a consistency of length of rein between hand and bit - unlike nylon reins, which are too soft and stringy thus producing variations in the contact. Likewise, plain leather reins are just a little too thin for me and can become slippery when wet or when the horse's neck is sweaty.

For my taste, bridles should be as simple as possible. I favour smaller, raised straps across the forehead and nose to enhance the horse's head, rather than the flat, broader type that can appear heavy. I mostly use flash nosebands as these close the horse's mouth effectively yet cause as little interference as possible with the air passages. The top strap can be fastened quite tightly to close the jaw above the bit, thus allowing the bottom strap to be just snug and therefore not affect the action of the bit in the mouth. Unless a dropped noseband is an absolutely perfect fit then the action of the bit can be affected.

With Messiah and Ricochet, who naturally tend to carry their heads high when approaching show-jumping fences, I sometimes add a fluffy, sheepskin shadow roll to their nosebands in order to encourage them to lower their head and focus their attention on the poles ahead. Usually I reserve this little bit of additional assistance for special occasions so as not to lessen the effect and meanwhile continue to try and school the problem out of them.

I am not against the use of running reins at home for corrective training in both show jumping and dressage schooling. Provided they are used to prevent a fault occurring rather than as a short cut to establish a false way of going, they can only be looked upon as constructive. For example, if I was experiencing problems with a particular horse coming up above the bit during canter transitions, I would use running reins to prevent this happening. If the horse does not come up then the running reins need not be applied and once this lesson has been learnt they can be removed altogether.

Running reins are also useful when galloping or during interval training with horses that are included to become a little excitable. They have the two-fold benefit of keeping them round, and thereby working them more productively from a muscle-development point of view, as well as reducing the likelihood of leg injuries caused by striking into themselves.

Whenever I ride at home, even when just hacking, I like to put protective boots on the horses' legs in order to prevent injury. A lot

I am not against the use of running reins as a training device if they are used correctly, as in this photo. They should be used to prevent a fault occurring rather than to force an outline.

of people put boots on their horses' legs when they are in the field, but this is something I don't do (my reasoning is explained in Chapter 8). However, when they are being exercised I insist on boots as it is then that the risks are substantially increased.

For show jumping, my horses wear open-fronted tendon boots to protect themselves from possible damage to the tendons, perhaps from their hind shoes. The shins remain exposed, though, so that if a horse decides to become a touch complacent with the poles he will feel his mistake.

When galloping at home and when cross-country schooling I always bandage my horses' legs, at least the front ones, in preference to wearing boots. I believe that bandages provide a combination of protection and support. This was something I learned whilst involved in flat racing some years ago. During that time I also discovered the benefits of using a cushion of air as an insulator against the inevitable knocks. By using bandage padding (like Fybagee) under elasticated bandages, the air contained within the padding will disperse a direct blow over a wider area, so reducing the intensity of the impact to any one point. For many years I placed my faith solely in this method and bandaged my horses this way for all their competitions. Then one year, at Burghley, Delphy Dazzle (wearing only Fybagee under his bandages) received a blow severe enough to prevent him from appearing in the final day's show jumping. Since then I have continued to use Fybagee pads but in conjunction with additional leg protectors under the bandages.

Over-reach boots offer useful protection to the coronary band and help prevent injury to the heels. I tend only to use them on the cross-country but not in the show-jumping phase as I suspect that they could offer too much cushioning to careless feet.

As standing martingales are outlawed in competition I some-times resort to a running martingale (which is permitted), although I am not a great fan of this device. I have discovered that occasionally it can produce an adverse effect, as was the case with Messiah when we tried one on him. Restriction can be the greatest cause of resis-tance, and as the rings of the running martingale are actually attached to the reins I sometimes find them prohibitive to the soft contact desirable. I much prefer a standing martingale, which is attached instead to the cavesson part of the noseband and is there-fore less interfering. I will often use a standing martingale during schooling sessions, especially when show jumping. Until the martin-gale is brought into play it is totally influence-free.

A good-fitting saddle is definitely most important. For dressage I prefer a deep seat that sits evenly on the horse's back with as large an area of contact as possible. This way as much weight as possible is well distributed, preventing any significant areas of intense pres-sure. If a rider has just one horse then it should be possible to fit his saddle to that particular animal. Unfortunately, when dealing with several horses it is impracticable to have a separate saddle for each one, so I employ a jelly pad or similar saddle pad underneath to compensate. This must not be overdone, though, or the rider could find himself perched so high above his horse that his seat aids would be of little consequence.

I have always show-jumped in an American-style flat-seated saddle. These have simple flaps under the leg to allow a close contact with the horse's side. I used to ride across country in the more traditional deep-seated, high-cantled, bucket-type saddle, incorporating the usual knee-rolls. I always thought this design would be difficult to fall out of - until, that is, I rode in my first ever European international event at Chantilly, France, in the summer of 1989. As I unpacked the lorry I realised to my horror that I had left

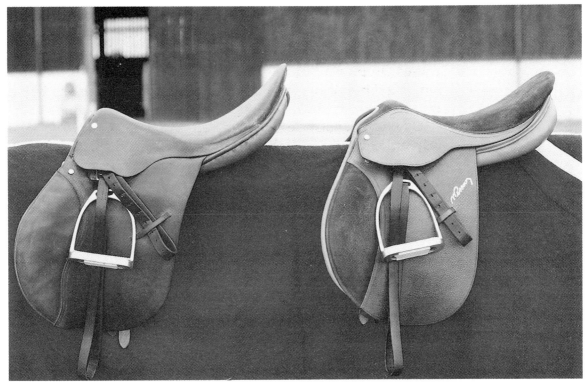

My old and new cross-country saddles compared. I used to think that the deeper-seated one on the left would help hold me in place and stop me falling off, until I discovered the flat-seated Pessoa on the right, which revolutionised my cross-country riding. With the Pessoa I have found that the closer lower leg contact and the freedom for upper body flexibility gives me the basis for far greater security.

my cross-country saddle behind. Being relatively new to the scene I did not know any of the other riders well enough to ask if I could borrow a saddle from them. Angrily I resigned myself to having to tackle the biggest track that I had so far encountered in my flat saddle. Feeling certain that I had jeopardised my chances of staying on board I was pleasantly surprised and now look upon my memory lapse as a blessing in disguise. I enjoyed the best ride imaginable and since then have never reverted to the high-cantle model. The lesson was well learned.

My new-found security was not so much the result of 'seat of the pants' riding, but more to do with the fact that the saddle allowed me to clamp my lower leg in place and still retain the flexibility and freedom to alter the upper body sufficiently in order to stay in balance. When riding across country it is necessary to be able to sit back and absorb drops and yet still be able to get forward for wide ditches or steps and banks in an unrestricted manner - and this saddle gives the rider the complete freedom to adjust his position as necessary.

The flat saddle also certainly saved me from a ducking in the 1990 World Championships in Stockholm. At the middle element of the Pleasure Pond complex, I found myself getting into difficulty on the Normandy Bank. Messiah produced an amazingly athletic and courageous effort to extricate us from our problems and keep going. I was able to throw up one arm and lean right back to stay on board. I feel sure that I would have received a dunking had I been held forward in a more bulky or restricting saddle.

I never ride - except perhaps in the dressage arena - without a breastplate. To some extent it is like driving a car without a seat belt, especially when the possibility of a slipped saddle is magnified by the inclusion of a necessary weight-cloth when competing at the upper levels. A surcingle or overgirth as additional security is also a must during competitions.

The only other schooling equipment that I use on a regular basis are the chambon and side-reins, which I put on when lungeing. With the volatile type of thoroughbred horse that I tend to favour, lungeing is a useful way of helping a tense horse to relax before a flatwork schooling session or dressage test. The chambon exerts gentle

Lungeing with a chambon - a device which exerts gentle pressure on the poll - will encourage big, relaxed movement. It also assists with correct muscle development. As can be seen here, when the horse's head and neck are lowered, the chambon ceases to come into play.

 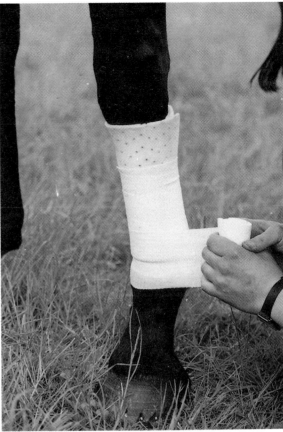

LEFT It is sensible to have a wide range of studs for use in all kinds of weather. I like to use only one stud on the outside of the front feet to reduce the chances of injury. The stud shown is positioned halfway down the shoe, and not at the heel where, if a hind foot catches the stud, the result could be a lost shoe.

RIGHT When going cross-country I prefer to bandage the horse's legs to offer both protection and support. The leg is first wrapped in a thin Fybagee pad, then enclosed in a hard-shelled leg protector (Porter boot) which is secured by an elasticated bandage (sewn in place for three-day competitions and taped for one-day events). It is important to apply an even pressure when bandaging, and to avoid over-tightening on the back of the leg.

pressure at the poll to encourage a long and low outline. This assists with the correct muscle development as well as promoting big, loose movement. Side-reins, on the other hand, can help in establishing a correct and secure outline and good balance.

A wide selection of studs should be kept on hand for use in varied weather conditions. When the ground is firm I like to use small, pointed, spike-like studs to break up the surface and provide some grip. This is even more vital when there has been a recent shower of rain on top of firm going, making the footing slippery. In

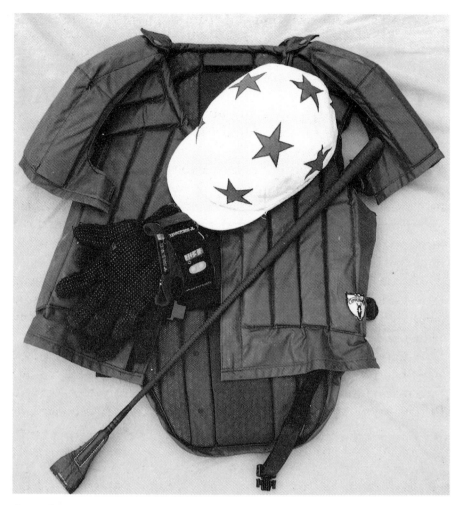

Some of my equipment for the cross-country: a well-fitting back protector with shoulder-pads; woollen gloves with rubber-pimpled palms; crash helmet and silk; an easy-to-read stopwatch; and rubber-gripped whip.

soft mud or heavy ground, large squarer studs are required.

I only ever use one stud in each front shoe, and this is screwed into a ready-made hole halfway up the outside face of the shoe. Here it is out of harm's way. I don't like to use a stud on the inside of the front shoe for fear that the horse could strike into himself, causing injury. Nor do I like a stud to be placed at the heel of the front shoe as this can increase the likelihood of the shoe being torn off by an over-reaching hind foot. I am, however, happier about using two studs at the heels of back shoes to maximise traction, but still tend to put a slightly smaller one on the inside to reduce the risk of injury.

Once the studs are removed from the shoes, the holes are plugged with cotton wool to prevent the thread from being ruined or the hole becoming blocked by stones and mud. When studs are next required the cotton wool is removed carefully with a horseshoe nail.

A quality, safety-tested and approved body-protector is an absolute must, and in most countries it is (quite rightly) compulsory to wear one on the cross-country. I use a top-of-the range protector because I am fully aware of the risks involved in this sport. Shoulder pads and additional spinal protection are provided as extras, and here again we find that the construction incorporates air to cushion and disperse impact. If well fitted, these body protectors need not hinder a rider's performance, and I have become so accustomed to mine that I feel positively naked without it.

Obviously the same requirements for safety are needed in head gear. I like a crash helmet that covers well down the back of the head and has an outlet for trapped air to escape through, thereby reducing the possibility of concussion.

Whips and spurs are a matter of personal preference. I carry a short whip for the show jumping, and a longer, rubber-gripped one for cross-country (it is not permitted for any whip to exceed 30 inches). I wouldn't contemplate going cross-country schooling or competing without a whip and spurs as you can never predict when you might need them.

I prefer to wear reasonably short, blunt spurs, and find that long or sharp spurs can leave their mark on the sensitive skin of the thoroughbreds I ride. Spurs should never be worn with their shanks pointing upwards as this is not only harsh but also a dangerous practice.

With most spring and late autumn events taking place in cold weather, riding gloves are a necessity. Not only do they keep you warm but they can also increase the sensitivity of the feel you have on the horse's mouth. Even in hot weather I still choose to wear woollen gloves with rubber-pimpled palms as these stop the reins becoming slippery when the horse's neck becomes sweaty. Undoubtedly, the blame for one of my worst cross-country rides can be put down to the fact that I wore leather gloves in the rain. This was a BIG mistake as the reins were constantly being pulled through my hands, resulting in loss of steering and control.

I have never been able to get used to the foreign feel of fingerless gloves, so I wear full-fingered ones instead; and for dressage I prefer white or light-coloured gloves.

A good-quality, reliable and sturdy stopwatch is the final accessory that completes the ensemble. Mine is worn at an angle on my hand to make it easily readable whilst I am galloping. To make life simpler it has a large display face with big digits. It is important that the stop, start and reset buttons require a firm press to activate them, otherwise the watch can trigger into action or stop itself when knocked during the rough and tumble of a cross-country round.

8

IN ONE END...
OUT THE OTHER

———————— • ————————

AS FAR as possible the general stable management and feeding methods that I adopt for my competition horses echo those of a horse in its natural environment.

If it were feasible I would prefer not to bother with stabling at all. In fact in New Zealand, where the climate and natural resources are more suitable, horses have been trained successfully for both racing and eventing directly from the paddock. However, in England this is just not practical and by stabling at night we can also more easily monitor a horse's fitness levels and feed intake. To compensate I like to turn my horses out for as long as possible every day. I feel it to be a great asset to their peace of mind, and it is also of immense benefit to their physical well-being.

During the course of five or six hours of free grazing, horses will roam a considerable distance while they randomly move about choosing which piece of grass to eat next. This exercise must make a useful contribution towards the stimulation of muscles and good circulation of blood. A similar time spent standing in a stable munching on a haynet must have less benefits by comparison.

I believe that the open air proves more conducive to clean respiratory tracts and it is good for the horses' digestive system to take food gradually over a period of time. Also, by eating with the head at ground level any congestion in the sinuses will be encouraged to clear.

If a horse is excessively greedy, as is the case with Delta, then I would first try to find it a suitably bare paddock before resorting to locking it up. Only rarely do I find this to be a problem with fit thoroughbred horses as usually the additional exercise enjoyed out

I like to turn my horses out whenever possible and for as long as possible. They always go out in company, wearing good-fitting rugs and no boots.

grazing serves to counterbalance the problem. Mainly it is horses standing idle in a stable with large quantities of hay that will convert the bulk food intake to fat.

I do not worry if my horses choose to run around or play in the paddock. Many people, however, would immediately rush out and catch the horses for fear of injury. I see this activity simply as a display of well-being, and it is a natural instinct for horses to run free. I tend to find that it is only when the horses are extraordinarily fresh or have been cooped up for a while that they will bother to run about much anyhow.

I turn my horses out in company with others, either in pairs or in small groups. Horses are herd animals and I find that they do best for being allowed to socialise. It only seems to be when horses are constantly kept separated for long periods that they will tend to develop anti-social or aggressive behaviour once they are reunited. However, I would not advise that mares and geldings are mixed together in any great numbers, and obviously most entires will need to be kept on their own.

I never bother to put boots on my horses' legs when they are turned out in the field. I prefer instead to give the legs ample opportunity to catch the exposed air, whether it be a cool breeze or warm sunshine. I believe that leaving their legs unprotected in the field helps the limbs to become just that little bit more resilient to life's little knocks. As long as the fencing is of a good standard and the paddock is free of hazards I am willing to take my chance. So far, touch wood, nothing untoward has occurred, so I see no reason to alter what I and the vast majority of New Zealanders consider to be normal practice.

When out in the paddock, if it is at all cold or wet, then the horses will wear good fitting, wool-lined canvas rugs complete with an additional neck rug extension. These will keep them warm and dry but will not prohibit their movement. In sunnier weather they will wear much lighter canvas sheets with neck attachments to stop either the persistently annoying flies or, as is the case in New Zealand, the harsh ultra-violet rays from the sun. Occasionally, when the weather permits, I will remove the sheets and allow the more mild sunshine onto their coats and backs as the sun offers an invaluable source of vitamin D.

I never cease to be amazed by the curious practice of keeping horses well rugged in the stable and then removing the rugs and turning the horses into the field naked - regardless of the weather conditions. Surely these extreme and sudden changes must be upsetting to the animals' metabolism?

If the weather is very hot or the flies too much of a nuisance, as can be the case for periods during the middle of summer, then I am quite happy to reverse the turn-out routine and bring the horses into the stable during the day and turn them out at night.

Because my horses receive ample opportunity to fill up on bulk when grazing, I feed very little hay, sometimes none at all. During the winter months and early spring, when grass is less readily available, I will feed plenty, but during the height of the competition season I prefer instead to give only controlled amounts. I find that by providing a balance of grass and chaff, sufficient roughage is given to ensure a balanced diet.

In the final three weeks before a major three-day event, I wean my horses off hay altogether. Top athletes do not fill their stomachs with bulk before an important race but instead refine their diet. My horses are athletes too, and I also feel that this practice helps to clear

	per scoop	OATS (recently crushed)	COARSE MIX	EVENT PELLETS	BARLEY (micronised)	CHAFF (lucerne)	Electrolytes	Garlic	Gen. Supps.
Private Benjamin 16.3hh, 11 years, Irish part-bred. Solid build. Relaxed temperament. Competing Adv ODE, approaching 3-star 3DE.	AM	1	1			$\frac{1}{2}$		√	
	PM	1	1		1	$\frac{1}{2}$	√		√
Perhaps 16hh, 7 years, NZTB. Average build and temperament. Competing Nov/Int ODE.	AM		1	1		1		√	
	PM		1	1		1	√		√
Ra Ora 16.2hh, 8 years, NZTB. Lightly built. Excitable. Lacking condition. Competing Int/Adv ODE, approaching 2-star 3DE.	AM			1	$1\frac{1}{2}$	1		√	
	PM		$\frac{1}{2}$	1	1	1	√		√
Messiah 16hh, 14 years, NZTB. Typical blood horse. Competing Adv ODE, approaching 4-star 3DE.	AM		1		1	1		√	
	PM	$\frac{1}{2}$	1		1	1	√		√

A typical feed chart for a cross-section of my horses during the competition season. An extra half scoop of bran is fed twice per week (Wednesday/Sunday).

1 scoop oats/barley/mix = 1.25kg/2.75lbs

1 scoop pellets = 1.5kg/3.3lbs

their windpipe completely from any dusty particles. I must admit that when I drive into a three-day event and see other riders unloading copious amounts of baled hay, I begin to feel a little guilty knowing that I have brought none. However, I insist that my horses are taken out to graze for long periods several times a day and find that this is more than adequate. The softer, more succulent grass is more readily digested and processed. I have yet to feel guilty at the end of a speed and endurance section because my horse has been excessively noisy in his breathing or overweight for the job.

If a horse tends to be particularly light framed or a slightly poorer doer then I will offer a horsehage product as a substitute. This is softer and more moist than hay and does not need to be fed in such bulky quantities. I always have some on hand to feed after the cross-country and on show-jumping morning.

My main objectives when feeding horses are to provide an appetising and balanced diet and to feed according to the amount of work being done and also the type of animal. I try to keep the regime as simple as possible but it is not always easy if the horse is a fussy eater, and each individual horse has different requirements. Initially - probably as a result of my racing background - I fed only straight cereals such as oats, barley and chaff, but I now use more mixes and pellets than previously with good results. I have found these types of feed to be less heating for excitable thoroughbred horses, such as Messiah and Ricochet, and yet they have not shown any loss of condition or energy. If I am feeding a reasonable amount of pellets, however, I always feed them with chaff otherwise they tend to pass through the horse too rapidly making the animal some-what loose in its droppings. For the same reason oats and barley should be well crushed before feeding or little value will be obtained from them. Unfortunately, oats will go off quickly if crushed too far in advance of feeding so if you don't own your own oat crusher it pays not to purchase in bulk. I find that boiled barley can help put weight on a light horse.

Horses that are prone to tying up (azoturia) should not be fed a meal that is very high in protein, such as found in oats and barley, but instead will do better on lower protein pellets and mixes.

I like to feed bran, which is a good laxative, twice a week, usually dry, adding it to the normal quantity of feed. However, sometimes after a particularly strenuous work-out, or the night following a competition, I will feed it as a bran mash, warm and mixed with either molasses or honey to make it extra appetising. I always place the warm mash on top of the feed to allow the horse to enjoy the mash before it goes cold. I do not mix it into the rest of the feed. I find mashes useful for disguising hidden extras, such as electrolytes or additives, which can be added to the hot water and molasses.

I tend to feed only twice a day except in the winter when the horses are stabled for longer periods. They receive one feed in the morning and another in the evening around 6 o'clock. I find it is not necessary to offer a midday meal when the horses are out in the field all day. However, it is worth remembering that considering its overall size the horse does not have a very large stomach and so it is not wise to give vast quantities to a horse in one feed. Consequently

I give a day's ration in two feeds of very similar size.

Every horse receives daily a vitamin and mineral supplement, which I believe to be of vital importance. Nearly every soil or pasture, if tested, would show a deficiency of some trace element or mineral. By feeding a general multi-vitamin and mineral additive the horse can take into the body whatever is required and naturally excrete the surplus.

By blood-testing a horse on a regular basis it is possible to discover any deficiencies or build-ups of unwanted substances in the horse's system. I have my horses blood-tested every six weeks during the competition season and more frequently still if recommended by my vet. That way any obvious change in well-being will show itself immediately. Blood-tests are also very helpful in showing up the degree of a horse's fitness and the presence of any viruses. A vet can very easily spot any abnormalities in the horse's blood, such as an undesirably high volume of white corpuscles (indicating infection), poor sedimentation rates or a below par haemoglobin count (suggesting a lack of fitness). Given this knowledge I can ease up on the workload until corrective measures are taken - for example, by the administration of multi-vitamins or antibiotics.

Some of my horses have specific additional minerals for various reasons: e.g. biotin to help promote the healthy growth of feet, selenium in conjunction with vitamin E for blood stability. I have also had a lot of success with feeding magnesium to horses who excessively and suddenly flick their head. I believe they do this as an allergic reaction to stinging pollen particles transported in the air and hitting the sensitive parts of their nostrils. Most people who are magnesium deficient also tend to be irritable by nature and very susceptible to allergies such as hay fever and asthma; and many show improvement by taking magnesium tablets. Head-flicking seems to be most prevalent in the spring when pollen levels are at their highest and appears to be increasing in intensity as more crops of rape-seed oil and the like are being planted. If not stopped early on it can eventually become incurable as the horse becomes psycho-logically upset by the feel of raindrops and flies etc., anticipating a stinging sensation.

I find that garlic, although it adds an unwanted smell to the feed, is useful for fending off coughs and colds and is good for the circu-lation in horses that might be suffering from minor joint creaks and muscular pains. Despite the odour, most of the horses still seem to enjoy the taste.

I try not to mix additives together, if at all possible, as combining certain trace elements can reduce their effectiveness. Thus I feed some in the morning meal and some in the evening to maximise their values.

I also regularly feed electrolytes, in controlled amounts, throughout the height of the season to counterbalance dehydration. After a heavy work-out with excessive sweating it is necessary to put back into a horse's system salts lost from the body via the sweat. Electrolytes will also encourage the animal to drink good quantities of water thereby replacing fluids to the body.

Mostly my horses are stabled on straw. This is mainly for purely

My horses are stabled on straw beds, which are laid right up to the door and have banks around the walls for cushioning. Every day, after mucking-out, the beds are put up to dry while the horses are out in the paddocks. They are re-laid again each evening. I like the beds to be at least a foot deep. Ricochet is tucking into his hay, which I place on the floor (never in a haynet) by the door.

practical reasons although I do believe it to be the cleanest type of bedding to work with and muck out. First and foremost, however, it is considerably cheaper than alternative forms of bedding such as shavings and paper, which, when running a large string, has to be a consideration. If laid fairly deep it offers an attractive 'mattress' for the horse to lie down on and sleep.

Although fully aware of the supposed ill-effects of the microscopic spores that are contained in straw I am not unduly concerned about them and believe that they are less harmful than the dust that inevitably comes off shavings. I remember being somewhat taken aback at an overseas event when I was given a severe lecture on the ills of bedding on straw by a well-respected and undoubtedly infinitely more experienced person than myself. Apparently the damage I was causing would be irreversible. Although I was not convinced, I was in no position to argue. I simply said thank you and continued to lay the bed. Just over a month later Messiah, still sleeping on straw, became World Champion, and he has continued to be bedded on straw ever since.

For the sake of convenience many people tend to sweep the bedding well back from the door, leaving a substantial space of concrete in the front of the box. I would not recommend this unless perhaps a thick soft rubber mat was laid across the area as it is most likely that the horse will want to stand in this spot to look out over the door. Standing on hard concrete for long periods can make the front legs susceptible to swelling.

The feed mangers and water buckets should not be hung too high if the horse is to be able to feed in the natural, head-down position, which allows easy consumption. Likewise, when I am feeding hay I put it on the floor rather than use a haynet. I would not risk hanging a haynet low down for fear of a horse's hoof becoming entangled in it.

On a day-to-day basis I try to stick roughly to a yard routine whenever possible, but invariably it alters from time to time due to competitions, lessons or other commitments.

On a normal day the horses are fed at 6.30 a.m., watered if necessary, glanced over and then left for an hour to digest their breakfast in peace. At 7.30 the day's exercising and mucking-out duties begin. Following work, the horses are allowed to cool down and are then turned out in the field for the rest of the day. If it is not possible to work any particular horse until later in the day then it will be turned out in the field first, straight from the stable.

In the afternoon the horses return to the stable and are thoroughly groomed before being put to bed. Although I said that the horses are kept as naturally as possible I am nevertheless very particular about paying attention to detail. After all, small problems can grow into major headaches. Whether it be a rug or boot rub, a scratch, a loose shoe, a dull coat or whatever, the problem is dealt with at the earliest opportunity so it has no chance to escalate into something worse.

Grooming is an integral part of promoting good health, and although it is mainly done to ensure cleanliness, I consider it to be just as beneficial as good feeding and exercise. When the horses are getting fit in the spring or are still competing at the tail-end of the season and are growing a thick coat, then they will be clipped. Too thick a coat will be a hindrance when working as it will cause too much sweating, making it difficult to dry a horse off or keep it clean. It is better to clip out the coat and add an extra blanket. I always clip my horses right out except for a small saddle patch. If I clip during the winter or early spring then I might leave the legs on for warmth, but once serious work begins then the long leg hairs will come off too.

Whilst the horses are being groomed and readied for bed, they are given any additional treatments they need, such as massage, pulse magnetic field therapy, whirlpool boots or whatever. I have only just discovered the value of massage now that I have a slightly better understanding of the muscle structure of a horse and the way in which particular muscle groups work. I am lucky enough to possess a hand-held vibro-massage machine but it is quite possible to be nearly as effective with simple finger kneading and wisping. Each of my horses has different areas that need constant attention to alleviate soreness or stiffness, either from working incorrectly or as a result of minor conformational defects. Messiah, for example, benefits from massage to the base of his neckline; Ricochet is worked on just behind the saddle area; and Ra Ora towards the back of his rump.

Whenever possible, although I don't actually own one, the use of a pulse magnetic field blanket can be helpful. When fortunate enough to be on the New Zealand team our vet has provided one for the team's use which gives a more overall muscle toning.

Also I like to make use of whirlpool or jacuzzi boots, especially after a hard competition or gallop. These can help to reduce any swelling or soreness due to concussion or bruising and can be used in conjunction with ice to disperse unwanted heat. If it is not possi-

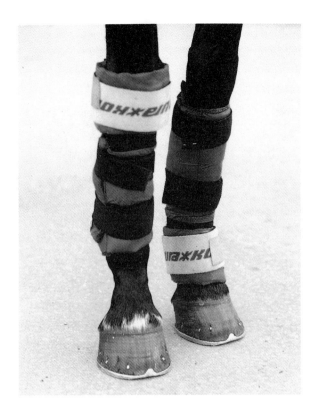

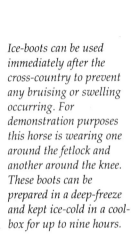

Ice-boots can be used immediately after the cross-country to prevent any bruising or swelling occurring. For demonstration purposes this horse is wearing one around the fetlock and another around the knee. These boots can be prepared in a deep-freeze and kept ice-cold in a cool-box for up to nine hours.

ble to use whirlpool boots then a cold running hose can be pretty effective but considerably more time-consuming.

Similarly, immediate application of ice to an affected area can also prove useful to prevent further bruising or swelling from arising. If the problem is in a limb, the ice can often be secured with bandaging. However, care must be taken when dry ice is applied directly to a leg as scalding can occur. This can be avoided by placing a thin layer of cotton wool between the skin and the ice. Nowadays there are some useful ice-boots on the market that can be frozen and will retain their coldness; others are fitted with special pockets to hold ice.

9

KEEP FIT

I DON'T believe it is necessary to make the conditioning of an event horse into a complicated and scientific procedure. I would suggest instead, and especially for the novice rider, that it is important to remember just a few basic principles. First, insist that the horse is sufficiently fit for the level of competition intended; second, insist that any increases in workload are very gradual; and third, do not be too rigid in your pre-conceived plans for your fitness programme.

There are bound to be occasions when it will become necessary to make slight adjustments to your programme to absorb the inevitable set-backs caused by minor injuries, loss of form, cancelled events or personal crises. It may even be sensible to increase the intensity of work if the horse shows a rapid acceleration of well-being.

It is important for a horse to be sufficiently prepared only for the level of proposed competition, so it should not be necessary for a green or young horse to follow the same fitness programme as an older horse preparing for an attempt on Badminton. Instead some thought should be given to trying to preserve a young horse and reduce any unnecessary wear and tear upon its limbs. The very nature of our sport asks for a high degree of physical effort from our horses, so any chance to prevent overdoing the demands on any horse should be encouraged. However, as a general rule of thumb, if a horse is heading for a three-day event it would be more desirable for the horse to be too fit than lacking in fitness.

For a part-time rider who is participating in a few novice one-day events, virtually any consistent daily exercise of about an hour's duration will probably prove sufficient, but for the more ambitious

A event horse's fitness programme must be built on a solid foundation of roadwork and hacking. This type of exercise can be used to promote condition or as a form of relaxation. Where possible, I will make use of grass verges in preference to unforgiving road surfaces.

who are targeting a three-day event, a more carefully thought-out and intense preparation will be needed.

When I first started out in eventing I tended to be fairly regimented in my pre-planning but now that I have more experience I rely more on my own judgment and discretion. Even so, I will still sit down with a calendar at the beginning of the season and set about mapping out a programme that will culminate in a targeted three-day event.

At this point it is a good idea to work out your schedule of fitness backwards from the date of the proposed goal to the beginning of the preparation, jotting down any prospective competitions that you might hope to take part in.

If a horse has been completely rested then I would want to allow at least seventeen or eighteen weeks for complete preparation and would aim to achieve peak fitness at least one week before the commencement of the three-day event. This will ensure that I am left with sufficient time to back off pushing the horse during any moments of concern, or, if all has gone well, then I shall simply be able to maintain the level of fitness, reducing the pressure I am exerting as the competition draws near and therefore leaving a little in the tank for the competition itself. I also might want to keep something in reserve to take account of the associated stresses of travelling, which to foreign events can sometimes involve considerable distances.

It is not possible to outline a programme that would be suitable for every horse and rider, as so much will depend on the type and breed of horse, and also on the time and commitment the rider can achieve. Personally I rely on a combination of traditional methods, more modern interval-training techniques and even some ideas borrowed from the training of racehorses. It suits the light-framed thoroughbred horses that I tend to ride and fits in with local terrain and amenities.

I start by laying a solid foundation of fitness that consists initially of steady roadwork and hacking exercise before incorporating the interval-training techniques. If the horse is completely unfit then the initial two weeks will consist of about an hour's walking. Gradually this will increase, but rather than prolong the period of time that I exercise my horses I tend to increase the intensity of the effort asked, by trotting. Very rarely do I ever work my horses longer than about an hour and a half. Once the horse has begun trotting I will begin to look for some hills to introduce gradually, so again the effort is increased slightly.

At this point I am happy to work on whatever surface is available but if given a choice I would prefer to work mainly on grass. However, in the spring when the ground is often excessively wet it is not always possible and so some roadwork is acceptable. When on tarmac I will mostly walk, but I won't rule out the occasional slow trot, particularly if the road incorporates a slight incline. I will only do this with care and with the knowledge that the road surface is not slippery and likely to cause an accident. Never do I risk trotting downhill on the road. The value of the inclusion of some work on a firm, flat surface at this stage of the preparation is that it can help to assist in the hardening of the hooves and strengthening of the bones,

as long as it is done in moderation. Never do I overdo the speed but prefer instead to contain the horse at a slow trot for fear that the constant impact might encourage a concussive effect and cause jarring.

During this initial stage of laying this solid base I will also begin to introduce some simple flatwork sessions a few days a week. This will encourage the development of some muscle tone as well as improve suppleness and obedience before any further strenuous exercise is undertaken.

If the horse was not already receiving any hard feed before his preparation began I would commence feeding him at the start of his work and would continue to do so according to the amount of work that was being done. As the work increases so does the amount of food offered.

Having now completed the first phase of the fitness programme, taking four to five weeks to do so, I usually feel that the horse has reached a sufficient level of well-being to begin a more serious training schedule. This will involve stepping up the cantering periods and thus starting to work on the horse's respiration as well as continuing to improve his muscle development. For this I like to rely mainly on an interval-training method, which involves timed bouts of cantering which become progressively longer and more demanding as the horse becomes fitter.

Perhaps the most beneficial aspect of interval training is that the amount of stress that we place the horse under is increased only gradually and the horse is given sufficient time to recover before being stressed again. Thus the likelihood of asking too much too soon is reduced and with it the risk of causing any damage is minimised./It is possible with this system easily to monitor these periods of stress on the horse and immediately to recognise the benefits or spot problems.

I plan the canter (or stress) days loosely around a four-day cycle, but inevitably, because of the calendar of competitions and various other commitments, I can't always stick rigidly to this schedule. Sometimes I will extend the period between canters to five days. By structuring the stress days four days apart, then hopefully any injurious side-effects will either be detected or will repair sufficiently before any further stress is endured.

Usually I will start with three five-minute periods of steady cantering, each canter being interrupted by three minutes of walking. I find that the horse will be either fully recovered or very nearly

FACING PAGE
Cantering Ra Ora during an interval-training work-out at home.

recovered by the end of the walk period, before beginning the next canter. With interval training being directly based upon the concept of stress and recovery it is an ideal method of fittening in relation to a three-day event, which makes the same demands. This applies not just to the speed and endurance, where the steeplechase precedes the cross-country, but also throughout the whole competition where having a fresh horse for the show jumping on the last day is vital. Producing the latter has, I believe, been the downfall of many riders who have performed dismally in the stadium on the final day on horses who normally, when fresh at a one-day event, jump clear rounds.

Gradually the periods of canter will be slightly extended but the rest periods of walk remain at three minutes. Ultimately it will be the level of the proposed three-day event and the type of horse that will indicate the length of canter periods to be eventually achieved. If the horse is heading for a four-star event, where the demands are at their greatest, these canter periods could easily reach three sets of twelve minutes each. However, for a young horse aiming at his first three-day event, then three sets of about nine minutes would probably be more than enough, remembering again the desire not to cause any unnecessary wear and tear.

If the horse has a tendency to be lazy or is perhaps a little more commonly bred, then I will try to work him alongside another to cajole him into trying harder by providing some competition. By gradually increasing the periods of canter we will be also slowly expanding the demands placed upon the limbs, heart and lungs, which will eventually serve to increase their efficiency. I do not worry too much about being over-technical in analysing heart beats and respiration rates but prefer instead mentally to note whether the horse's breathing is excessively heavy or if he is taking a prolonged time to recover. Soon it is possible to recognise what is normal for that particular horse and to notice improving recovery rates.

Where I am based it is most practical for me to execute my interval training around the outside of a large flat field, which is quite adequate for the task, but if I was able to incorporate undulations or uphill pulls I would reduce the length of the cantering accordingly. At least by working in a circular fashion I am able to complete each timed canter without interruption.

On the intervening days between the cantering sessions, my horses will continue with their flatwork, their hacking and jump schooling. For me, hacking serves two purposes. It can either be looked upon as an opportunity to condition or as a form of relaxation and gentle exercise after hard work such as a competition or canter day. Normally then I would allow the horse to go mainly in walk on a loose rein and unwind mentally and physically. Otherwise I would continue to do trot work with the horse engaged over varied terrain (sometimes quite hilly ground) to further strengthen and develop muscle tissue and to enhance stamina. During this time I still like to make the work as enjoyable as possible and will frequently pop the horse over the odd ditch or log that might be encountered.

It may be necessary, for the continued expansion of the horse's respiration system, to complete some additional speed work. This is of particular relevance to one-day events, where speed is more of a requirement over a shorter distance (as opposed to the slower, more sustained effort of a three-day event). Some horses are naturally much more clean-winded than others, so again the amounts of speed work can be quite varied. I give my horses a short pipe-opener twice a week, two days apart, based upon the old New Zealand racing theory that if Saturday is race-meeting day then Tuesday and Thursday are for fast work-outs. However, as the season progresses and after a few events are completed, the frequency of these gallops between competitions is reduced. I like to try to complete the gallops on an uphill run if at all possible in order that the distance covered should not be too great for the benefit of their limbs and yet the effect on their wind is still retained. These pipe-openers can work in conjunction with the canter sessions, which would then probably be reduced in duration for that day (see sample fitness programme overleaf.)

It is always worth remembering the old saying, 'Speed kills'. How often do we hear of horses breaking down in walk or trot? Virtually never. How often in a slow canter? Very rarely, and yet in gallop it is quite frequent. A bowed tendon or a major breakdown can very seldom be put down to sheer bad luck. More often than not it is the result of bad management. A breakdown will occur where there is a lack of oxygen supplied via the bloodstream to operating tendons and ligaments, causing the elasticity of the tendon fibre to rupture. Thus breakdowns are most likely to occur when a horse is over-exerted too early or when the horse is tired and unable to sustain the required effort. Of course, it is quite possible for a horse to twist or strain a leg when landing awkwardly over a fence or on uneven ground, but still I would ask myself whether the horse was

25 Grange field

A   B   C   D   E   F   G

A	B	C	D	E	F	G
Jan 26 hack 1hr, walk/trot	**27** hack 30mins, dressage school 30mins	**28** hack 1hr, including hill work	**29** hack 1hr, mainly trot	**30** hack 1hr, mainly walk	**31** dressage school 45 - 60mins	**Feb 1** day off
2 road work 1hr	**3** hack 1hr, including hill work	**4** lunge/school	**5** hack 1hr, mainly trotting	**6** dressage school 45 - 60mins	**7** hack/jump school	**8** day off
9 road work 1hr	**10** hack, including some cantering	**11** hack 30mins, school 30mins	**12** dressage lessons (staying away	**13** at trainer's)	**14** hill work, trotting, a little cantering	**15** day off
16 road work 1hr	**17** hack, mainly trot	**18** lunge/school	**19** dressage show	**20** hack 1hr, mainly trot	**21** hack/SJ school	**22** show jumping show
23 day off	**24** dressage school	**25** dressage show	**26** road work 1hr	**27** hack, including canter	**28** hack, including hill work	**March 1** day off
2 *5.3.5.3.5	**3** light road work	**4** dressage school	**5** hack 30mins, school 30mins	**6** *5.3.5.3.5	**7** hack, light jump school	**8** show jumping show
9 day off	**10** *5.3.5.3.5	**11** lunge	**12** dressage lesson	**13** hill work, mainly trotting	**14** *5.3.4.3. pipe opener - 600m three-quarter gallop	**15** road work (light)
16 show jumping lesson	**17** hill work, mainly trotting	**18** *6.3.6.3.6	**19** lunge/dressage school	**20** dressage 1hr	**21** *6.3.6.3.6	**22** day off
23 hack 1hr	**24** hack 30mins, dressage 30mins	**25** *4.3.4.3 pipe opener - 600m gallop	**26** dessage 1hr	**27** pipe opener - 1000m three-quarter gallop	**28** hack 30mins, school 30mins	**29** COMPETITION
30 day off	**31** road work 1hr	**April 1** hack, mainly trot	**2** *7.3.7.3.7	**3** lunge/dressage school	**4** show jumping lesson	**5** dressage school
6 *7.3.7.3.7	**7** road work 1hr	**8** hill work, including some canter	**9** dressage 1hr	**10** *5.3.5.3 600m gallop	**11** hack 30mins, school 30mins	**12** COMPETITION
13 day off	**14** day off	**15** road work 1hr	**16** hack, mainly trot	**17** *8.3.8.3.8	**18** hack (light)	**19** dressage
20 hill work, mainly trot	**21** *8.3.9.3.8	**22** hack 30mins, SJ school	**23** show jumping show	**24** hack 1hr	**25** *9.3.9.3.9	**26** road work
27 dressage school	**28** dressage school	**29** *9.3.9.3.9	**30** day off	**May 1** hack 30mins, school 30mins	**2** COMPETITION	**3**
4 day off	**5** hack 1hr	**6** lunge/schooling	**7** *10.3.10.3.10	**8** hack 1hr	**9** dressage school	**10** dressage/jump school
11 *10.3.10.3.10	**12** travel to event, hack at venue	**13** trot up, early hack, evening school	**14** DRESSAGE	**15** DRESSAGE pipe opener	**16** CROSS-COUNTRY	**17** SHOW JUMPING

* = interval training work-out. Note that the figure 3 always refers to walk; the other figures always refer to canter.

Fitness/work schedule for an average advanced horse heading for a three-star three-day event. The chart assumes that three to four weeks of walking and trotting have already been completed. If flexibility is needed, build it in on the days between interval-training work-outs, and try to keep the cantering sessions as scheduled. I would not be unduly worried if a horse missed a few days' work, but I would be concerned if he missed a week or more.

satisfactorily fit to enable it to withstand such an occurrence in the first place. A fitter horse will land more lightly and gallop more athletically and consequently will be more likely to save himself.

On the evening following a gallop, a canter session or a competition, I pay particular attention to the horse's limbs. Normally, also, the following morning the horses will be trotted up in hand. If any visible swelling is in evidence, any muscle soreness is noticeable or there is any detectable increase in heat in the legs, then immediate action is taken. The workload and heating food are reduced straight away and steps are taken to alleviate the problem by the application of ice, or ultra-sound or some other therapy, as explained in the chapter on stable management.

I like to give the horses at least one full day off per week, which they spend at their leisure in the field. With younger horses I don't even mind if they miss the odd additional day too, as they tend to hold their fitness more easily.

When choosing the competitions that I wish to take each horse to I will select the ones that will best fit in with their fitness programme and will help to prepare them for their ultimate goal. With the older horses I like to space these events out and also include dressage and show-jumping outings so they don't begin to anticipate a good gallop every time they appear in public. With the younger horses I tend to compete them more frequently in order to complete the necessary mileage to acquire experience, but if so I will work them much less at home in between times.

Many of the lessons I have learnt have regrettably been taught the hard way. I can vividly recall the one occasion when I had a horse break down on me, and with hindsight now making me wiser I can see the errors of my ways. The fact that the incident happened to Ricochet, probably the most generous, genuine and kind of all my horses, makes it an even more bitter pill to swallow.

It happened during the spring of 1991 when I was preparing Ric for his first attempt on Badminton. Earlier in this chapter I suggested that it is important to be flexible - with Ricochet in 1991 I was not. I was adamant that he should stick to his pre-planned cantering regime despite the fact that the ground was excessively wet. Consequently, despite wearing protective boots, he managed to strike a blow to his near suspensory ligament, causing swelling and bruising to the area. He was required to miss some vital work whilst the swelling was reduced with the aid of laser therapy, and once able to resume work I sped up his workload slightly in order to catch up.

When a horse's work programme is interrupted for any reason, swimming can be substituted so that his overall fitness does not suffer unduly. This strenuous form of exercise offers an opportunity to continue work on respiration and muscle development without burdening the limbs. Before Badminton in 1992, Ricochet (pictured) and Delta swam twice a week in addition to their normal interval-training regime.

However, at his very first event, Brigstock, possibly as a result of transferring some of his weight from his previously sore near fore-leg, a bow to his off-fore tendon resulted. Clearly I had not prepared him sufficiently, and trying to run him quietly across country was no help. Ricochet is very bold across country and didn't want to be restrained when so fresh. Given the opportunity again I would defi-

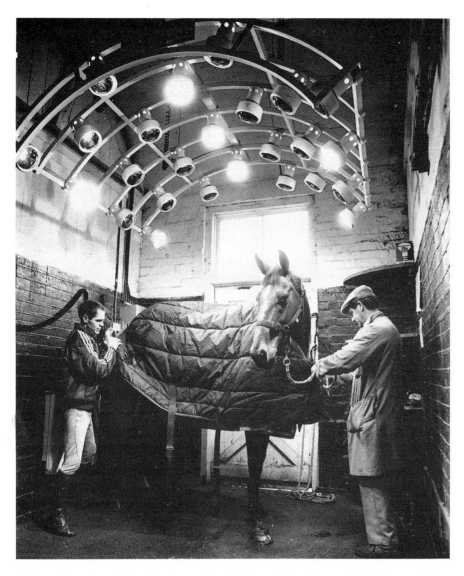

Infra-red heat lamps help Ricochet to dry off after a swimming session. He is now being rugged up for the journey home.

nitely do things differently.

Right from the start it would have been sensible to seek alternative ways of building fitness when the ground I had to work on was unsuitable. A possibility would have been swimming, which I have since used successfully. Under normal circumstances I would not wish to rely solely on swimming as the only ingredient for fitness as eventually the horse must bear weight in competition, but as a temporary saviour or additional extra it can be quite useful. It is said, however, that swimming in circular pools can lead to uneven muscle development as the horse is constantly turning. If so, I feel this can be counter-balanced by working in both directions and I'd be more fearful of the horses building up the under-muscles of the neck and creating a hollow top-line as a result of holding their head above water.

Alternatively I could have simply backed off and waited until Ric's leg was settled and the weather had improved enough to allow a continuation of a full programme before participating in any competitions. As it was I achieved nothing constructive and missed Badminton anyway. It is much easier to be wise with hindsight.

10

REMEMBER TO LOAD THE HORSE

———————— • ————————

WHEN I first started competing in one-day events I thought I had a pretty good idea of what I should take with me in the lorry and how I should conduct my plan of attack. Over the years the list of 'essentials' has grown to proportions that resemble a tack-shop inventory - and I have found out the hard way that nothing sharpens up your memory or makes you review your methods like learning from your mistakes. Although I am grateful that I forgot to take my cross-country saddle to my first major international competition, I would rather have made my discovery about the advantages of flat saddles in a panic-free zone! Nowadays I have a 'belt and braces' approach to packing my tack and equipment, and I would never, for example, not walk a course thoroughly, or walk one casually, even if I had ridden at that competition before.

Items to take to a one-day event

The following list is based on one novice horse competing at a one-day event.

- Bridle and spare bridle.
- Jumping saddle.
- Dressage saddle.
- Breastplate - elasticated is preferable for cross-country.
- Martingale - if the horse requires one.
- Martingale stoppers - be sure to have rubber stoppers for the reins to prevent the martingale rings becoming entangled in the buckles.
- Surcingle.
- Change of bits.
- Spare halter/headcollar.
- Saddle cloths - at least two in case

Messiah in the ten-minute box, awaiting the start of the cross-country. He is wearing an elasticated breastplate and surcingle to secure the saddle. Under the saddle is buckled a weight-cloth. He is bandaged all round, and his legs are greased so that they can slide over the fixed timber fences should he make a slight mistake.

one becomes sweaty, dirty or rain-sodden.
- Fybagee - four pieces for the cross-country and at least two spare.
- Tendon boots for show jumping - open-fronted.
- Porter boots - these are not self-fastening boots but leg protectors designed to be worn under cross-country bandages.
- Over-reach boots - rubber, slip-on ones, for use on cross-country only.
- Exercise boots - for warming up before dressage or for hacking about.
- Exercise bandages - optional.
- Stable bandages - plus under-wraps, e.g. large Fybagee

squares.
- White cross-country bandages - four.
- Tape - to secure bandages (at three-day events the bandages will be stitched as well).
- Tail bandages.
- Lunge line and whip.
- Stable rugs.
- Sweat sheets.
- Rain sheet.
- Warming rug.
- Spare shoes.
- Ice boots - kept in cooler box for application immediately after cross-country.
- Plaiting kit - including needles, thread, rubber bands, scissors and comb.
- Stud kit - including spanner, studs, tap and horseshoe nail to remove cotton-wool plug.
- Mucking-out gear - if an overnight trip.
- Haynets.

- Feed buckets.
- Water buckets.
- Boot lace to secure bridle to top plait.
- Sponges.
- Scrapers.
- Grooming kit.
- Saddle horse.
- Bridle rack.
- Towels - plenty.
- Uptite poultice.
- First-aid kit.

For the rider
- Stopwatch.
- Back protector.
- Riding boots.
- White gloves.
- String gloves.
- Cross-country sweater.
- Cross-country hat.
- Show-jumping hat.
- Jodhpurs.
- Whip.
- Spurs.

Items for the ten-minute box at a three-day event

I have included this list as people are always curious to know what I take into the ten-minute box. With so many items it is important to lay them out in a neat and organised fashion so it is possible to find, say, a replacement stirrup leather or a safety pin at a moment's notice. On paper, the list looks very long but all the items below can be easily transported in just a couple of big canvas bags.

- Spare saddle cloth.
- Spare breastplate.
- Spare martingale.
- Spare girth.
- Spare surcingle.
- Spare bridle.
- Spare reins.
- Stopwatch.
- Whip.
- Gloves.
- Stirrup.
- Fybagee.
- Halter/headcollar.
- Sweat sheet.
- Blanket.

- Rain rug.
- Towels.
- Buckets.
- Sponges.
- Scrapers.
- Hoofpick.
- Ice wraps.
- Ice.
- Scissors x 2.
- Hole punch.
- Gamgee.

- Animalintex.
- Arnica cream.
- Dettol.
- Cotton wool.
- Bandages.
- Wound powder.
- Spare shoes.
- Stud kit.
- Event grease.
- Plastic gloves.
- Vaseline.

- Safety pins.
- Boot lace
- Needle and thread.
- Martingale stoppers.
- Pen and paper.
- Porter boots.
- Exercise boots.
- Tape.
- Over-reach boots.
- Spare cross-country bandages.

Competition tips

On the pages that follow I have noted down a few tips and reminders, and organised them into the chronological sequence that would occur in the course of going to a one-day event.

Travelling to the event

✦ When driving the vehicle try to decelerate into corners and gently accelerate out of them as this will give the horse a better ride. Make no sudden directional changes or stop or start abruptly as this will unbalance the horse and could cause him to lose his footing.

✦ In cold weather, try to keep the horses reasonably warm by putting on rugs, but still keep the vehicle well ventilated. In hot weather keep the horses cool - maybe travel them without rugs - and, of course, keep the vehicle well ventilated.

✦ Use good travelling boots or bandages for protection.

✦ I don't like to offer hay or hard feed when actually in transit as I fear the horse could choke if he is unable to have free access to water (which in a lorry is not possible).

✦ Shavings or straw on the floor during long journeys will help encourage the horses to stale normally.

✦ If travelling some distance, perhaps even overnight en route to a competition, don't feed immediately on arrival. Give the horse a

Messiah is given a final polish before our dressage test at Badminton. This is done well in advance of performing the test so that the final working-in is uninterrupted.

walk to stretch his legs and allow him a pick of grass; feed at least an hour after unloading.

Arriving at the event

✦ Quickly familiarise yourself with the layout of the venue so you know the distance to the dressage, cross-country and show-jumping disciplines.

✦ Find out if a blacksmith or vet is in attendance and, if so, how to locate them.

✦ Perhaps show the horse around a little to assess his attitude to his surroundings.

✦ Collect numbers and confirm times early.

Working in for the dressage

✦ Having tacked up in plenty of time, ride around the warm-up area for a while before getting down to work. Don't expect immediate attention from the horse.

✦ If necessary, a quiet lunge can be useful to relax and iron out any early kinks.

✦ Try not to prolong the working-in with a novice or it will set the standard for the rest of his life.

✦ Try to peak at the time of your test by calculating your working in. I like to loosen up, ask for a little obedience, practise a few movements, remove the boots and tidy up the horse; then I return to working for the last ten minutes before the test to maintain the flow.

✦ If things are going very well it may be necessary to 'back off' for short periods and perhaps relax on a loose rein to avoid going 'over the top'.

✦ Learn the test well in advance so that you are confident you are familiar with it. If you fear that your memory will be overcome by the atmosphere, have a copy of the test handy for a last-minute refresher.

✦ Know where the judging of each movement begins and finishes so you know where it might be more possible to score a ten.

Riding the test

✦ Be practised in arena-craft.

✦ When riding down the centre line ride positively forward with your eyes up. It is easier to go straight like this than if you dawdle or meander slowly.

✦ Ride only as deeply into the corners as you can without spoiling the overall rhythm.

✦ Show definite transitions. I find that if the horse has not been as responsive as well as I had hoped in the lengthening stride, for example, a good transition back at the end will discourage the judge from being able to say 'No lengthening shown'.

◆ Ride good shapes by looking up and ahead and by being well practised.

◆ Don't worry if you botch one movement. It's done. Get on with the next movement as there are still points to be scored.

◆ When in the arena, try not to ride too differently from the way you would in training. The horse will know if you are beginning to freeze. Correct mistakes at novice level and cover them up at championships.

◆ Prepare in advance for each movement or transition and then flow on. Looking and thinking ahead will help this happen and will assist with accuracy.

Show jumping

◆ Be sure to walk the course thoroughly, taking note of related distances and measuring combinations. Most courses will be laid out on the basis of 12-foot canter strides (four good-sized human steps) but the ground conditions, gradients and the type of fence could influence these distances. You should already be aware of your horse's stride length and will know when more or less pace will be necessary.

◆ Be aware of fences in relation to the collecting ring or entrance. Note any particularly spooky fillers or surroundings.

◆ Try to watch a few other competitors ride their rounds. Any major problem fences usually tend to present themselves.

◆ Don't overdo the jumping in the warming up. I find that half a dozen fences jumped off both reins is normally enough.

◆ Save the medium trot for the dressage. Warm up to jump with a slow, more controlled, rounded stride.

◆ Trotting a cross-pole first can help settle the rider's nerve and start the horse off gently. You will get an indication of your horse's attitude by the way he copes with this initial cross-pole. If he is over-confident or over-enthusiastic he may need more jumping than if he is bored by the whole affair.

◆ Again, try not to be ready too soon and risk going 'cold' in the last

Normally I start my show-jumping warm-up by popping over a small cross-pole. This gives me an indication of how my horse is feeling and I can then judge how much working-in he needs.

ten minutes before you enter the arena. If possible, have someone watching the ring proceedings to let you know how long until you compete. I like just a few minutes after my last practice fence to check girths etc. and recite the course route, then I move into the ring still warm.

Walking the course

♦ Try to go alone or with one advisor or fellow competitor and concentrate. It is not a time for a picnic or a gossip with friends.

✦ If walking the course the day before competing, it can be a good idea to walk at about the same time of day as your cross-country round. Make a mental note of where the sun might be, as well as shadows etc.

✦ Choose the lines or options that you imagine will suit your horse best, not the lines that everybody else thinks you should take. Only someone who works closely and regularly with you can speculate on your own and your horse's preferences and abilities.

✦ Look for the most direct or economical route between the fences but also pay particular attention to the footing. The quickest line is not always the best.

✦ Look back from time to time at the previous fence as you walk to

When walking the cross-country there are many factors to bear in mind. I concentrate on the best options for the particular horse I'm riding, taking the opportunity to pace out distances in combinations and visualising each fence from the horse's viewpoint.

the next to ensure that you are not straying from the most direct, ideal line.

✦ Be aware of all the alternatives and flag positions and walk each line in case you need to make an unscheduled change to your initial plan.

✦ Watch the numbering of each fence (especially important in combinations), to avoid missing fences out or unnecessarily retaking parts of a combination that you have already negotiated.

✦ Before setting out to ride the course, I always mentally run through the entire track, imagining each approach and counting each fence in succession.

✦ Try and visualise the whole course as one unit and sort out where the hills are and any slow, winding sections. Some sections may ride a little more easily so at these you could perhaps press on; if there is a significant incline towards the end, you may need to conserve some energy.

✦ Make a decision and try to stick to it. Don't dwell on the consequences too much or it won't promote attacking riding.

Riding the cross-country course

✦ Do not rush straight out of the start box and try to be in top gear by the time you reach the first fence. By all means start positively, as that is how you will want to continue, but gradually increase your pace once you have found your rhythm.

✦ Try to flow from start to finish, so that the horse can establish a regular breathing pattern. By varying the pace dramatically, for example by repeatedly sprinting and slowing, the horse will tire sooner.

✦ Safety is of paramount importance. Ride in an attacking manner but do not take unnecessary risks. Always hope for the best, but expect the unexpected.

✦ Try to teach yourself to wear a watch at novice level in practice for a three-day event. Good timing and judgment of pace can be self-taught. I now automatically glance at my watch intermittently around the course so I'm always aware of the time I am taking. However, do not ride against the clock just to score points,

Leaving the start box. I am particularly careful at the first fence to ensure that the horse is paying attention, and once safely over the jump I think about moving up into a higher gear.

regardless of the effect it will be having on a novice horse's education. Ride only as quickly as safety permits.

✦ If wearing a weight cloth (at higher levels) make sure that it is securely fastened to the saddle so that it cannot work free. Distribute the weight evenly in front of and behind the leg. Some people like to put most weight over the horse's shoulders, which does indeed ensure that the 'dead weight' is central to the horse's balance when galloping, but it also puts extra weight onto the front legs, possibly causing jarring or injury.

Finishing the cross-country course

✦ Try to keep some petrol in the tank for the end of the course, especially if there are difficult combinations towards the end. It is better to start too slowly and build up momentum than to start too fast and tire.

✦ Always remember, however, that a few time faults are preferable to jumping penalties. At novice level, exceeding the optimum time is not considered a crime. It is a time for building a confident and rideable horse for the future.

✦ When pulling up at the end of the course, do so slowly. I always take a good time to reduce to canter, trot a few yards and then walk. It is when pulling up abruptly that horses can often injure legs and muscles.

After-care

✦ Don't let the horse 'cool out' too quickly. Cover him up and keep him walking around gently until his breathing has regained some normality.

Sponging down after the cross-country on a hot day, to remove sweat and help cool the horse. Excess water is scraped off and the horse is dried with towels before being walked in hand in a sweat sheet.

✦ Sponge him down and scrape him off, and if it is cold, cover him up whilst still walking him around.

✦ If he has had a bump and cautionary ice is to be applied, then straight away is the time to do it. Ice will assist in preventing immediate bruising or swelling.

✦ Some homeopathic remedies, such as arnica tablets and creams, can be very helpful in relieving bruising and the like and will not test positive against rules.

✦ Offer only small drinks to begin with, increasing the amounts gradually as the horse recovers more fully.

✦ Don't offer feed too soon after competing. Again, a light pick of grass would probably be appreciated.

✦ Finally brush off and make comfortable with appropriate rugs. The legs can be kaolin poulticed in an attempt to draw any heat or strain. First apply the poultice, then surround the leg in damp brown paper before bandaging over the top. The paper will help to keep the poultice moist for longer.

11

VIVA BARCELONA!

————————— • —————————

THE Olympic Games are most definitely something quite unique. They are unlike any other international three-day event in the world. At times the pre-Games media hype can border on the excessive, and public awareness, too, rises to a crescendo. Even the most unhorsey of folk suddenly become patriotically supportive of their homeland riders in their quest for much-coveted medals.

During the run-up to the 1992 Barcelona Olympics I did my best to shut out all the hullabaloo and its associated pressure, for fear that it could detrimentally affect my planning and performance, and to some extent feel that I did succeed. But far more difficult to control was the self-imposed pressure to do well: with the Olympics being staged only once every four years I knew this could be my first and last opportunity.

My 1992 spring campaign had been relatively successful, and much boosted by a chance meeting with Philip Billington that led to the signing of my first serious sponsorship deal, with the UK-based company, Toggi Ltd. This good fortune allowed me the luxury of travelling to the Continent to gain my Olympic qualifications at the slightly less-taxing Saumur and Punchestown events, therefore (thankfully) by-passing the unfortunate and difficult weather conditions that prevailed at Badminton in 1992. Furthermore I was lucky enough to be chosen for the New Zealand team with two horses, Ricochet and Messiah.

A week before the start of the competition the horses were boarded onto a plane and flown to Barcelona. We had anticipated that the weather would be hot and did not want to arrive in Spain too far in advance of the competition. It was felt that a week was sufficient time for the horses to recover from their journey and to acclimatise to their surroundings.

FACING PAGE
Into the second water complex, with grit and determination. Messiah, Barcelona, 1992.

The stable block for the Olympic horses was a brand-new, specially built, split-level construction, designed in the shape of a triangle with a central courtyard. Fortunately the New Zealanders were allocated some outside stables on the second storey. These faced the valley beyond and therefore enjoyed any slight breeze that was available. We were thankful that we were not stabled with the Brits and Americans, who were accommodated inside the courtyard, which was hot and airless.

The working facilities were criticised by many as being inadequate, but I felt they were quite sufficient for my needs. Due to the 'mañana syndrome' that prevailed throughout the Barcelona Games, the sand surfaces were not put into the dressage working-in arenas until the competition was actually under way.

Communication was certainly a problem, though, as I found out when I accidentally broke the rules. Because there was very little grass available within the compound I suggested to my groom, Delayne, that she take Messiah and Ricochet for a pick of grass outside the compound where scarce amounts could be found. However, I forgot to warn her to be back before seven o'clock in the evening. Delayne, thinking she was doing the correct thing, stayed out as long as possible only to find on her return that the gates had been locked and the horses were refused re-admittance. It took much hair-pulling and anguish to convince the stern-faced guards, who understood nothing about horses and no English at all, to let the horses return to their stables. The guards would have been quite happy to let the horses stand outside the compound all night.

The three-day event was staged at El Montanya, about 80 kilometres away from the heart of Barcelona, where the Olympic village was sited. Since it was to prove difficult for the riders to travel out every day to the horses, the New Zealand team went to the considerable additional expense of renting a house (costing around US $5000 per week) just a couple of kilometres away from the stables.

The day after our arrival was taken up by quietly working the horses. I was on my way back to the stables having exercised Messiah, when he became momentarily excited by a roadside machine and launched into his usual favourite antic of cantering on the spot. Unfortunately, during his acrobatics he trod rather heavily on a sharp stone. For a couple of strides he held his foot off the ground in pain. However, after a further four or five strides he returned to walking normally. Once back at the stables I reported the incident to our team vet, Wally Neiderer. Precautionary measures were taken

immediately, tubbing the foot and putting on leather pads with silicone underneath to reduce the likelihood of bruising the sole again.
There seemed no further cause for concern.

That evening the opening ceremony for the 25th Olympiad was
to take place, and I had been adamant all along that I very much
wanted to attend. To me, taking part in the Olympic Games meant
participating in the opening ceremony, and this has always been one
of my biggest desires. We were bundled into buses and transported
into the city for the opening, but from that point on my illusions
were somewhat shattered. Although the Spanish had gone to great
lengths to stage a flamboyant and spectacular show, the participating athletes were unable to see any of it. Instead we were shepherd-
ed about, initially to the Olympic Gymnasium and, later, had to
stand under the main stadium grandstand, waiting for our cue to
appear on the track. True, that moment was exciting, but I am not
sure whether it over-rides my memories of aching feet and clinging,
sweaty clothes.

I still hadn't decided which of my two horses I should ride. Ricochet, on the one hand, had the better recent track record. He had
gone well in the spring, winning at Milton Keynes; he had also won
his Olympic qualifying three-day event at Punchestown in Ireland.
After that he had just one more run - in the final selection trials for
the British team at the Savernake Horse Trials - and yet again he had
shown excellent form and won. Messiah, on the other hand, had
been a little more difficult to get into stride that spring, having had
the whole of the previous year off with a minor injury. But Messiah
was the proven horse with four-star mileage. So initially I was very
open-minded - that was, until I walked the course. Instinctively I
knew that the track had been built for Messiah: the combination
distances were long, the straight routes very bold, the going was
certain to be hard, and the temperature hot - all the things that
Messiah seems to relish. Ricochet, however, much prefers going
with a little less of a sting and enjoys shorter striding distances, so I
knew that the course wasn't going to suit to him so well. So after
both horses had passed the first trot-up the decision was therefore
made that I would ride Messiah. Ricochet went immediately on a
free holiday!

Messiah's dressage had not been too brilliant that spring, but
after working with Hans Erik Pedersen we had just begun to arrive
at a reasonably secure stage. The night before his test was due to be
performed, I was exceptionally pleased with the way he had worked

under Hans Erik's guidance. Messiah had suddenly become very forward again, and a little lighter in the contact. His half-passes were particularly good, and I was even beginning to feel a little hopeful. I felt that all the hours of effort we had put into his preparation were beginning to pay dividends and that perhaps, after all, we had got the timing just about right.

The next morning I worked Messiah again, as I wasn't due to do my dressage until about five o'clock in the afternoon. Once more he went very well, although I was careful not to over-stretch him and had just hacked him about in the atmosphere of the competition arena. He then returned to the stables to be plaited and spruced up for his big moment.

As our time drew near I set off on the half-hour ride along the wooded path that led to the dressage arena. I began Messiah's final working-in. To my horror, I found him to be lame. All hell broke loose.

I was completely devastated and could not believe that this could be happening to me. It had to be a nightmare. With some urgency I had to locate the vet, the blacksmith and the *chef d'équipe* and relay to them the bad news. Without the support and encouragement of the entire back-up team, I'm certain I would have withdrawn there and then.

The team spun into action. My admiration for the talents of the blacksmith, Mick Fryatt, grew tenfold by the minute as he removed the shoe and replaced it several times in an effort to rectify the problem in Messiah's foot. The blame was laid on a shoe that had moved just ever so slightly while on the hack up to the arena. This had increased pressure on the previously bruised area, producing a severe reaction. The shoe came off, the pad came off; the shoe went back on again, but Messiah still looked uneven when trotted in hand. The pad went back on again, minus the silicone - still uneven. A little piece of his foot was pared off, the shoe replaced once more, and still he was uneven. We just didn't know what to do, and time was running out.

Jo Snelling, a previous working pupil of mine who was acting as general team groom, was despatched to retrieve ice and the laser machine. Unfortunately she had great difficulty in catching a shuttle but, ever-resourceful, soon found herself clinging to the back of a huge Spanish motorbiker travelling at terrific speed to the stables. (She swears to this day that she will never ride on a motorbike again.)

The foot was packed with ice and given as much laser therapy as time would allow. Meanwhile, my test was drawing closer and closer and I still hadn't done any working-in at all. I really didn't want to ride, but everybody cajoled me into getting changed. It was suggested that the extra adrenalin induced by the prevailing atmosphere would see Messiah through the test and that we could review the situation afterwards.

With only minutes to go I was legged up onto poor old Messiah, who had done no working-in at all and was obviously feeling some discomfort in his hoof, and ushered down to the arena. On the way I received some very strange looks from officials and spectators who had noticed that I wasn't previously mounted and was now about to enter the arena 'cold'.

Messiah's test was appalling, but how could I blame him? He was a victim of circumstance. Typically, though, he took full advantage of the situation and enjoyed what he thought was an incredibly fun time. Delighted, he blew a fuse completely. It was true, the

Trying to leave the arena after our appalling dressage test. Our prospects of a medal were now decidedly bleak.

adrenalin had stopped him feeling the discomfort in his foot, and tough horse that he is, he completed his dressage test without the uneducated being aware that there had been any significant physical problem. His trot work had been more painful for me than it was for him. I was totally unable to make him go forward - as he was far too busy gawping at all the spectators and having a wonderful time. The extensions were particularly difficult as he totally resisted the hand. Suddenly I thought, 'Oh my God, I'm actually up to the canter,' and I knew there would be little improvement. Canter is his most difficult pace to ride and when he's not completely worked-in and well connected, all he will do is swing his quarters and change legs frequently behind.

When the test was over I was very relieved to leave the arena. Immediately I was besieged by an enquiring press. I was unusually abrupt, which must have appeared rude, but how could I speak to them when I didn't really know what the situation was myself? And, of course, my first concern was to see to my horse. After arranging for him to be led back to the stables, I returned to face the press and relayed to them my obvious disappointment. We were to end the dressage phase in the hopeless postition of sixty-ninth.

That night, to put it mildly, I was both physically and emotionally crushed. Messiah's bruise was pin-pointed, and although we attempted to release the pressure from the area we never really found anything more than a spot of mild bleeding. It was touch and go whether he'd be able to participate further.

As I lay in bed that night my thoughts were totally negative. I decided that it was time to contemplate giving up. I had come so far and made so much effort, only to have the carpet pulled out from under my feet at the unkindest moment. I was devastated.

Undaunted, everybody else involved in the team remained one hundred per cent positive. We worked for the following couple of days to alleviate Messiah's bruise, and I must admit there was a noticeable improvement. But I still didn't know whether he would be able to run or not.

On cross-country morning there was considerable turmoil in my mind. The team vet, Wally Neiderer, was adamant from day one that Messiah would get better with each passing minute, and that galloping would in fact help the blood circulation in the foot and improve matters considerably. I was so disheartened I couldn't be easily convinced. Wally advised me to go for a ride and think things through. 'But in the end,' he said, 'it is entirely your own decision.'

I did go for a ride and I experienced a very hard time in coming to a decision. I had to weigh up very difficult choices. On one hand, I didn't want to let the team down; but on the other, I had a wonderful horse whom I didn't want to risk around a tough course, especially if there was no chance that he would finish the competition. By Burghley, only a few months later, the problems that were plaguing him now would be well and truly remedied. Should I save him for another day?

Hacking back to the stables Messiah started fooling around and cantering on the spot - and that alone made up my mind. If he was well enough to do that he was well enough to at least start, and I would take it from there. I told Wally I had made my decision. We would begin the competition, and if I felt at any stage that he wasn't right, I would pull up immediately.

Messiah was left in his stable and I joined the other team members in the ten-minute box to watch the competition unfold. Several people came up to say how sorry they were that I was having to withdraw. How bad news travels fast!

The course was causing its fair share of problems. However, our first team member, Andrew Nicholson, put in a brilliant display of tactical riding and gave New Zealand a great start with an outstanding clear round. Regrettably, that was all I had time to watch before returning to the stables to prepare for my ride. Once I was kitted out, Messiah was tacked up and we were ready to go - but inexplicably there was a sudden hold-up at the start at Phase A. We were unable to find out why. There was no news filtering through to us, and the TV monitor in the stables was screening swimming events and the American 'Dream Team' basketballers; there was no mention of what was going on the cross-country course. The delay lasted an agonising threequarters of an hour. Under normal circumstances it is bad enough waiting to start on speed and endurance day, but being held up for an additional forty-five minutes at the Olympic Games was a soul-searching time.

I can honestly say that from the moment we started on Phase A Messiah did not experience even one slightly unlevel step. He was his usual unsettled self, pulling and jogging and wasting valuable energy, but he managed Phase B, the steeplechase, with complete ease. Messiah is a great galloper with a huge stride for a small horse, and being also a very careful jumper he found the unusually upright fences on the steeplechase to be no problem. He finished well inside the time, pulling up quite comfortably.

To me, Phase C always seems to go on forever, and at Barcelona it was no exception. However, an excellent new idea was implemented in this phase, due to the very hot weather. An extra stopping point was set up for washing or cooling down the horses. It seems to me that horses cool down in the first four or five kilometres of Phase C, recovering from their exertions on the steeplechase, but then they begin to sweat again soon after that and can come into the ten-minute box quite hot. Providing the luxury of an extra stopping point was an intelligent inception and invaluable in protecting the horses' well-being.

Arriving at the second stopping point, I was greeted by some very anxious-looking faces belonging to Wally and the support team. I assured them that all was still OK and after a quick sponge-down we continued on our journey. The ground jury had been informed that I had been experiencing problems with the horse, and were on hand in the vet box to see Messiah trotting in on arrival, and then again later in hand. I'm pleased to say he was passed as sound.

Vicky Latta had also gone exceptionally well for New Zealand so when it came to my turn there was nothing to lose. Lying sixty-ninth after the dressage it was vital for me to contribute to the team effort by attacking the course and finishing with a strong time, not simply to play safe and jump quietly around all the longer alternatives.

Messiah shot out of the start box with all his usual enthusiasm and was just a little headstrong and unsettled for the first five fences. At fence two I decided to jump on the right-hand side, whereas my team-mates had jumped on the left over the sloping garden option. In choosing the oxer on the right I was able to maintain a more sweeping approach, and with the aggressive manner in which Messiah usually sets out, I knew it would be the best alternative for me. It wasn't until about the sixth fence, the Sheepyard, that Messiah began to realise that he was not on a normal, everyday course but was in fact at the Olympic Games. When I had walked this fence I'd agreed with the other competitors that the distances between the combinations seemed quite long, so after gaining sufficient control on the turn, I rode strongly down the slope to the stride and bounce. I found that Messiah, never one to lack impulsion, jumped so boldly that we were nearly left with insufficient room for the four strides that made up the distance to the large table fence on the exit of the combination, which so many other horses had struggled to reach.

Jumping extravagantly out of the brush combination at fence eleven - still full of running and ahead of schedule.

I had been unable to look at my watch at the three-minute marker, which was just before the turn into fence six, but as I glanced quickly at my watch on the way out it read only two minutes fifty-five, and I realised that we were travelling at quite a considerable speed.

At fences ten and eleven, the circular double of brushes, Messiah was again slightly too extravagant and landed half-way down the bank on the landing side. At the five-minute marker that followed, I wasn't surprised to find that we were still twelve seconds up on the clock, although I had made a conscious effort to try and relax Messiah and slow him down.

We jumped through the most direct route at fence thirteen, the first of the water complexes, and although he jumped a little low over the ditch and wall on the way in, he still made up ground, only getting his final fourth stride in with a little shuffle before leaping up on to the bank, over the top of the barn and then down, off the other side. Here he drifted slightly to the right, although I had intended to be as far to that side of the fence as possible because the stride was slightly longer on the right-hand side and I knew that he would need the extra room. He jumped boldly in and immediately on landing in the water I had to pull hard left to prevent him from jumping the tall guardrails that surrounded the pond and which he mistook as the next part of the fence.

Making the turn towards the ski-jump, I was well aware of the problems it had caused previous competitors and knew that there had been several stops and even the odd spill. For once, I chose to over-ride Messiah and was perhaps just a little too strong. He was always going to jump it, having never before refused on a cross-country, so I don't know why I thought he would do so there. Having over-ridden him at the ski-jump I then lost control slightly as we careered down the hill to the big log suspended in front of the water. Because he jumped in so big, I had to slip my reins. I was rather untidy through the water and was struggling to regain the knitting in order to be sufficiently balanced for the exit fence.

By the twenty-first fence, he was still showing no signs of tiring, but I was. His constant pulling and extravagant jumping was taking its toll in the excessive heat. I had been in two minds as to whether to tackle the stone wall corner at fence twenty-one, or to take it in three efforts. Ultimately I decided that, as he was galloping so strongly, it would be easier for me to opt for the corner: holding him straight was going to be easier than attempting to turn him sharply.

At the next serious combination, the final water complex, I had always believed that the direct route would suit Messiah best. Now I was wondering if I should play safe because I was riding as a member of a team and not just as an individual. As he was still full of running, I considered it to be a calculated risk. Knowing that he was still on time, I chose to go over the direct route which only two others had attempted, and of which only one was successful. He made light of it, and the enormous applause from the crowd was unbelievable as we left the lake. This was all that was necessary to really set him alight again and send him on his way.

I had also been tempted to jump through the 'owl-hole' at the Owl Houses at the next combination, but on monitoring the fact that

Leaving the second water complex via the direct route. In my efforts to gather up the 'knit-ting' I let go of my whip, but luckily it became entangled in the reins and I was able to recover it.

the long alternative to the left-hand side took very little time and was predominantly risk-free, I decided that here discretion would be the better part of valour.

Galloping past the twelve-minute marker, I glanced at my watch once more and saw that I was still five seconds under the time. I began to entertain the thought that we would finish inside the opti-mum time. Soon after, I made the single, most stupid riding error of my life.

We were approaching the penultimate fence, a combination made up of wagons. I had decided to take the slightly longer right-hand route as per the rest of the team, and as I turned left-handed to take on the first wagon, I realised I was on a very committed forward stride, and kicking, asked for a slightly bigger jump. However, I then let Messiah continue on to the next oxer in this forward, long stride, when really I should have sat up quickly, checked and insist-ed on an extra stride being put in to make sure that I would land over the second part of the combination with sufficient control to negotiate the sharp turn to the right, for the exit. Such was our speed that it was immediately apparent that I wasn't going to be able to make the turn and avoid a possible fall because I would be asking for an extremely tight turn within the penalty zone on firm but slick ground. I tried instead to go straight ahead and pull up before turning behind a cluster of trees. However, there stood in front of us a five-foot barricade of metal fencing protected by wattle panels, to prevent horses from straying into the galloping lanes on an earlier part of the course on the far side of the penalty zone. Messiah mistook this for yet another part of the fence and bravely tried to jump it. I'm sure he would have succeeded cleanly too, if I hadn't been restraining him. Although he cleared it easily with his front legs he caught his back legs momentarily in the fence. After extracting ourselves from an entanglement of ropes, pegs and trees, and eventually finding an opening back onto the course, any chance of finishing inside the time allowed had completely evaporated.

Messiah galloped strongly through the finish flags and was still difficult to pull up even then, brushing past one poor person, who hadn't seen us coming, and knocking him to the ground (he did survive!). I had experienced a really fantastic ride from an incredible little horse, and although I should have been absolutely elated, I was left cursing my stupidity at making that silly error at the second to last fence and thereby incurring 8.8 totally unnecessary time penalties.

There was some satisfaction, however, in the knowledge that the home preparation must have been good, because Messiah seemed extremely fit and felt as though he could have gone on galloping at the same pace for several more minutes if asked. He appeared completely unperturbed by the run, and he was soon led back to the stables by Delayne, which was no mean feat in itself. Throughout the long walk he continued to dance and prance, squashing poor Delayne on numerous occasions.

Once safely back in the stables he was put, as is normal, in his whirlpool boots and soon after was trotted up in hand. He appeared to be showing absolutely no ill-effects from his exertions.

As it turned out there was further disappointment in store for the Kiwis. Welton Greylag, ridden by defending champion Mark Todd, broke down on the steeplechase and was not able to take any further part. Thus it had proved vital that Messiah had run. I owed so much to the rest of the team, and I still wonder how on earth I could have been so negative and selfish in my thoughts of not taking part.

Late that night Messiah still looked very good and most content. The next morning he passed the final vet check with flying colours. The galloping had improved his foot dramatically, as Wally had predicted. The horses were then trucked downtown into the Real Club de Polo showgrounds for the final show jumping. On arrival Messiah was randomly drug-tested.

The show-jumping course was very futuristic. Most of the fences were all of the same colour, and each depicted a scene from Barcelona, photographed and then stuck on to the fence. The course was laid out in a fairly deep sand arena, and I knew from my experiences at Stockholm that this could cause tired event horses even more difficulty, and that perhaps clear rounds would be even fewer than normal.

By this time Messiah had moved up to an unbelievable eighth position in the individual placings and I was beginning to think in a satisfied way that it wasn't too bad a performance after all, finishing in the top ten.

He wasn't exactly brilliant in the show jumping, as he was set alight again by the atmosphere. I took particular care at fence four, the double, because I had decided that this was a bogey fence, and he was very good, clearing both parts with plenty to spare and boosting my confidence somewhat. But turning back to the water fence, I left him a little under-revved, and was rather lucky he found some extra oomph and did not land on the back tape. I'd also been worried about the planks that followed the water jump, thinking he may be difficult to contain after the effort of stretching across the water. Thankfully I had a right-hand turn in which to regain control and therefore could set him up to jump the fence cleanly. He was a bit too quick through the treble, the second to last fence, gaining speed, but he managed to jump it cleanly, and then, just as in Stockholm, the crowd began to make a noise, and he started to accelerate towards the last fence. I had a real fight on my hands but just managed to hold him. He achieved sufficient height to clear the vertical fence and finish the round without penalty.

It was all over, and under the somewhat trying circumstances I felt we had given it our best shot. We could at least be proud that we had managed to complete a double clear round at the Olympic Games. Nevertheless I couldn't help thinking that here was a case of 'the one that got away'. Sure, anyone can say 'if only...', but at the time I felt that the cards had not exactly been stacked in our favour.

The Olympic show jumps were particularly unusual, both in colour and design. Each one featured a different photograph depicting a scene from the city of Barcelona. Messiah seemed quite unperturbed by their appearance.

I stood watching the remaining competitors perform their rounds. One by one they made mistakes, then suddenly I found myself being congratulated from all directions. It took time for me to realise that I had been elevated to third place individually and the bronze medal was ours. How indebted I was to my gallant little horse.

For poor Andrew Nicholson I felt much sympathy. He had performed so outstandingly in two phases, the dressage and the cross-country, only to experience a disastrous show-jumping round which dropped him right down the final placings. As a team member no one could have wished for a better trail-blazer. He had been incredibly supportive and helpful in letting his fellow riders know exactly how the course was riding.

I also felt sorry for Vicky Latta. She had been given ten penalties for a technical error at the last water complex and that was enough to rob her of a much deserved individual medal. No one is more meticulous in their preparation than Vicky and nobody works harder. To finish fourth must be one of the hardest placings to accept, being just outside the medals.

1992 wasn't to be Mark Todd's year either. As the defending title-holder he was mounted on a talented horse and was tipped to go into the record books as the first triple individual winner. He'd been having disappointments enough before the Games and Welton Greylag's lameness was yet one more devastating blow for him.

Despite all the set-backs - which would certainly have knocked back a less-determined and resilient nation - New Zealand battled on to the end to claim the silver, just missing out on a team gold by a whisker. Somehow I can't help thinking of the result as anything other than a victory.

MAJOR CAREER HIGHLIGHTS

1988
- 2nd Hawkesbury 3DE, Australia (Messiah)
- 1st Pukekohe 3DE, New Zealand (Messiah)

1989
- 2nd Achselschwang, Germany (Messiah)
- 2nd Chantilly CCI, France (Messiah)

1990
- Individual Gold Medallist, World Equestrian Games, Sweden (Messiah)
- 1st Scottish Open Championship (Ricochet)
- 2nd Badminton Horse Trials (Messiah)
- 5th Burghley Horse Trials (Ricochet)
- Winner L'Année Hippique Award

1991
- 2nd Luhmühlen CCI, Germany (Delphy Dazzle)
- 3rd Barcelona CCI, Spain (Shady Lane)
- 4th Werribee CCI, Australia (Mighty Express)
- Winner British Superleague ODE Series

1992
- Official World Ranked No.1
- Individual Bronze Medallist, Olympic Games, Barcelona (Messiah)
- Team Silver Medallist, Olympic Games, Barcelona (Messiah)
- 1st Punchestown CCI, Ireland (Ricochet)
- 1st Blair Castle CCI, Scotland (Tempo)
- 1st Scottish Open Championships (Ricochet)
- 2nd Burghley Horse Trials (Delta)
- Winner L'Année Hippique Award

1993
- 2nd Badminton Horse Trials (Ricochet)
- 1st Christchurch CCI, New Zealand (Mattson)

1994
- Winner Land Rover FEI World Three-Day Event Rider Ranking
- 1st Chantilly CCI, France (Just a Cracker)
- 1st Bramham CCI (Aspyring)
- 1st Boekelo CCI, Holland (Aspyring)
- 2nd Boekelo CCI, Holland (Just a Cracker)
- 2nd Badminton Horse Trials (Delta)
- 1st Scottish Open Championships (Delta)
- 3rd Necarne Castle CCI, Ireland (Perhaps)
- 4th Blenheim CCI (Ivor Chance)

INDEX

Page numbers in *italics* refer to illustrations.

PHOTO CREDITS

B/W PHOTOS: Stephen Barker - page 104, 110, 111; Barn Owl - 8, 10, 12, 13, 19, 20, 36, 52, 59, 117, 131; John Birt - 16, 22 (both), 25, 28, 30 (both), 32 (both), 33 (both), 34, 40, 42, 46, 47 (both), 71, 75, 76, 81, 83, 85, 86, 87 (both), 88, 92, 97, 100, 102, 114, 120, 121, 123, 124; John Blake Picture Library - 64 (both), 65; Expo-Life - 56; 'Les Garennes' - 51; Paul Green - 37, 53, 61; Anne Grossick - 66; Kit Houghton - 41, 77, 140; Bob Langrish - 2; Peter Llewellyn, 15; Trevor Meeks (courtesy *Horse & Hound*) - 68, 126, 137; Anthony Reynolds - 58; Barbara Thomson - 35, 135.

COLOUR PHOTOS: facing page 48 - Martin Dalby; facing page 49 - (top) Kit Houghton, (bottom left) Steve Yarnell, (bottom right) Kit Houghton; facing page 80 - Kit Houghton; facing 81 - (top left) John Birt, (top right) Trevor Meeks (courtesy *Horse & Hound*), (bottom) Shaw-Shot.